THE CODE OF THE WORD

An introduction to the
Universal Etymological Dictionary 1001 Words

The book "The Code of the World" by the outstanding Kazakh writer and philosopher Olzhas Suleimenov continues the collection of the books of classic Kazakh writers in English which Kazakh PEN-club decided to publish in the USA. The book collection "We Are Kazakhs" is being published under the supervision of the President of Kazakh PEN-club

MR. BIGELDY GABDULLIN

Classics of the Kazakh Literature

THE CODE OF THE WORD

An introduction to the
Universal Etymological Dictionary 1001 Words

Olzhas Suleimenov

Translated into English by Simon Hollingworth

КАЗАҚ ПЕН-КЛУБЫ

"We are Kazakhs"

Classic Books of Kazakh Writers in English

Metropolitan Classics Inc.
135 Ocean Pkwy, Suite 1U
Brooklyn, New York 11612

Copyright © 2016

All rights reserved under the International and Pan American
Copyright Conventions. Published in the United States
by Metropolitan Classics Inc., New York,
in the United States and Canada.

Cover design by Vance Klein; crosscheckdesigns.com

Suleimenov, Olzhas
The Code of the World – 1st American Edition
Metropolitan Classics Ed.

ISBN 978-1-57480-005-0
© O. Suleimenov, 2016
© Simon Hollingworth, Translation, 2016
© Design – Crosscheck Designs, 2016
Printed in the United States of America and Canada

TABLE OF CONTENTS

From the author 7
We set out in a search for ancient signs.
We encounter them on different paths 11
The smile of god 13
Priests 16
The First Rule 19
The Grammar of the Negative 21
A spear in the side - a sign of negation 23
Negation – diminution 25
The Second Outcome 26
Further to the above 27
Approaches to the *1001 Words Dictionary* 27
Rule IV 28
The fifth rule 29
Traces of the sign of the ox 31
Negation of the negation 32
Boustrophedonic letters 33
A full five marks 35
Alpha (novellas) 39
As far back as in Sumer? 42
How to turn ox into lion 43
Where did the ox go? 45
The ox gives rise to the elephant? 48
Cartwheels and flips of the ox 50
Yet another African 52
We wander to meet ourselves, recognising ourselves in others 53
The slave rab and the main arab 55
The philosophy of the beginning. the first opposition 57
The Epic of the Mountain of Grief Gora Gorya 60
Eastern Romance Language 63

The Syllabic Palindrome 65
Before Adam and Eve 66
Chinese Human 68
The Approach to Bowing 69
The Turkic Reading of the Chinese symbol for Human 70
How else can we express respect and veneration? 71
The Sumerian arrow is still in flight (about the great and the abject)... 73
Adam and Eve? 76
On Geniuses and Giants 77
Man with Arrow 78
Ah, Samara – what a town 80
In the Middle or on the Margins – Hittites and Hattites 82
The Man With an Arrow in Sumeria 86
The Knight and Mum 88
The Turkic Pyramid 90
The code of the word (a brief course) 96
Onomatopaeia (the simple symbols of moon worship) 96
Sign symbolism (from simple signs to compound signs) 97
Change in faith. The birth of the compound symbol 98

FROM THE AUTHOR

UNESCO has set about implementing a truly epochal project – the summarising of human knowledge about its history, from the time Homo Sapiens first appeared, 100-150,000 years ago in the equatorial region of East Africa. The first family grew and new families, clans, tribes and ethnoses emerged. The fight for survival forced humans to seek new places to live.

The stage of the great migrations of humans across the world is interesting in that the nomadic camps became the birthplace for the language from which thousands of dialects would then develop; a culture appeared, both spiritual and material. The Thinking Human became the Intellectual Human.

The age of human migration was completed recently, when state borders, protected by international law, were erected and the creativity of the Intelligent Human reached the highest levels.

Kazakhstan is financing the initial part of the project known as *The great migrations of humanity in prehistory and early history.* The first international conferences to shed light on this subject were organised by the Permanent Delegation of the Republic of Kazakhstan under UNESCO. In Paris in June 2008 one conference examined the starting points of the genesis of Homo Sapiens, their spread across Africa and the migration of separate groups onto other continents.

In the main hall of UNESCO's headquarters, geneticists, archaeologists, linguists, culturologists and anthropologists came together for the first time.

We held the second conference *(The Great Migrations: from Asia to America)* in New York in 2011, with the involvement of the University of Columbia.

The third will take place in Seoul at Hanyang University in 2013, titled *The Great Migrations: Southeast Asia and the Far East.*

Other similar events are planned, including one in Spain, pertaining to the settlement of Europe, and one in Russia, pertaining to the settlement of Northern Eurasia.

The last will be held in Kenya, from where it is believed humankind first originated.

Each conference will be followed by the publication of a collection of the speeches made there. The Kenyan conference will culminate in the publication of the *Atlas of the Great Human Migrations Across the Planet* and volumes of works that summarise human knowledge, supplemented and redefined thanks to implementation of UNESCO's global project.

We now afford great significance to the word as the key evidence of a prehistoric past. Based on names of localities, rivers, mountains and islands we can also map the routes taken by languages over continents and oceans. If we learn to read the word. And this is why the role of etymology grows ever more important.

The current, so-called *scientific etymology* has so far not departed far from what we know *as popular etymology*. This is because the same method is used, where the word is perceived only by its sound and on the uppermost, superficial layer of its meanings is understood. However, the two hundred year experience of *scientific etymology* has shown us that the deep-rooted beds of history of the word are inaccessible to the method of phonetic conformities. The linguistics toolkit needs supplementing, its origin enhanced with visual and poetic means and world-view insufficiencies done away with.

When contemplating the origin of the most ancient hieroglyphs (Sumerian, Ancient Egyptian and Ancient Chinese), I saw a link between the name of the figurative written symbol and its shape. Once the shape of the symbol changed, so its name changed immediately thereafter. Tracing this thought further in this direction

I detected a systematic nature in such transformations – an interesting interdependence of grapheme with name.

Half a century of my studies of this phenomenon have led to the discovery of the genetic interdependence of the First Language and figurative scripture (the sacred symbols of the Moon, the Sun and Venus). And, accordingly, to the recovery of the rules of the first grammar of the first dialects, from which all modern day languages have developed. Contemporary dictionaries indeed contain words that were created according to these rules. The language of scripture began to reveal itself to me; every first word was initially the name of a written symbol.

This is what *The Code of the Word* is about.

It is packed with subject matter for coursework, theses and dissertations. I set them out in sketched, outline form, knowing that a brief Japanese *tanka* or a four line Persian *rubai* can contain more than any multi-volume work. I was initially schooled as a geologist and my involved searching the mountains and steppes with a hammer, a search engine of sorts, looking for outcrops of minerals on the surface, chipping off samples and subjecting them to initial analysis. Exploration geologists would then return to this site to determine the volume of the deposit. I believe that I have now completed an important part of this initial seeking. Now I have to engage the readers who love the chemistry of the word to join me in working on a universal (meaning a polynational) etymological dictionary. A new etymology may indeed become a major supplier of historical information.

Dictionaries will helped any ethnos, large or small, to attain a greater understanding of their past, starting from the very origins. There is more historical truth in the content and structure of a verbal word than museum collections of skulls and precious jewels. The archaeological artefacts found during a dig beneath your home by no means belong for sure to your ancestors.

The written chronicles, too, go no further than several centuries. The verbal word has distinct advantages over the written document, albeit as yet unappreciated by modern science. The verbal word will not go up in flames and will not suffer from damp. It cannot be edited to suit a temple or a palace and it does not grow old. An ethnos may leave the historical arena and simply disappear, yet its words will live on in other languages. Dictionaries are an eternal and the most reliable archive of true historical information. They will be accessible to us if we can at last find that golden key to the Word. It will reveal to us the secrets of the origin of the Word and Scripture and that means the secret of language. A realisation of the interdependence of the Word and the Symbol is that golden key. This is what *The Code of the Word* is about.

New etymology will enhance people's respect for their native languages, something that, alas, is not accessible to most people today. A dictionary stores a great history even of the smallest, dying ethnos.

For reference

In the process of preparations for the 1001 Words, the author has published a number of books. These are a number of them:

AZ-i-IA, Alma-Ata, 1975 – 351 pages (Turkisms in Slovo of Polku Igoreve. Part Two – on Turkic-Sumerian language connections.)

Yazyk pisma, Rome, 1998 – 499 pages (On the origin of scripture and language)

Tyurki v doistorii, Almaty, 2002 – 319 pages (On the origin of ancient Turkic scripture)

Peresekayushchiye paralleli, Rome-Almaty, 1998-2004, 102 pages (On Turkic-Slavonic studies)

These works have been republished and released in different languages.

Olzhas Suleimenov – Ambassador, Permanent Representative of Kazakhstan at UNESCO

WE SET OUT IN A SEARCH FOR ANCIENT SIGNS.
WE ENCOUNTER THEM ON DIFFERENT PATHS...

In the beginning was the word,
and the word was with God...

This famous statement from the Gospel according to John, I think, expresses more accurately the Christian answer to the question of the origin of the word. And the continuation is *the word gave rise to all else – faith, culture, language and things.*

For some two and a half centuries science has been trying to work on its own answer.

A number of ingenious linguists-cum-codebreakers, who discovered forgotten languages and cultures in ancient writings, have extended the stairway into history by a few more millennia steps, reaching almost as far as the Neolithic Period. The Sumerian clay tablets, the ancient Chinese tortoise shells with engraved hieroglyphs, the papyri of Ancient Egypt and stone obelisks with the writings of the Ancient Turkic people are dispersed all over the world and yet they are in no way connected with one another. This tells us of the separate advent of each of these hieroglyphic systems, each independent of one another. The only thing that can unite them is a common faith, a worshipping of the Sun that prevailed until the advent of new religions across the globe in the first millennium before the Common Era, as far as America.

That said, the shapes of the symbols of the Sun continue to consolidate the general conviction that the cultures and writings of the Ancient World were independent of one another: in none of them, it appears, did the authors of the symbols, in creating a sacred sign, even attempt to render the written sun recognisable. While we can concur with the Ancient Egyptian spotted sun (⊙– Ra), on which the wise conclusion can be reached that even the sun has spots [*every bean has its black*], how are we to interpret the Ancient Turkic *half-sun* (D – jaj – *sun*), or the acute-angled Sumerian (➤ – ud – *sun*), or the Chinese square (⊟ – ři – *sun*)? If linguists or historians of scripture were for some reason to gather all these symbols onto a single sheet of paper, the resulting hotchpotch would be of use only to confirm the truth in the hypothesis of Ferdinand de Saussure: *L'arbitraire du signe* (1916). What he had in mind was both the word and the grapheme. Judging by his works, of all the forms of scripture, this University of Geneva professor was familiar with only letters and the literal form. Therefore, it is probable that he did not encounter symbols of the Sun, but it transpires that he did foresee their heteromorphism, which can only be explained by the arbitrariness of the decisions made by the authors of the various symbols. De Saussure's discovery went a long way to simplifying the work of etymologists and historians of scripture, who no longer need to root out the causality of the word and the graphic sign. All the etymologist has to do is present a picture of the spread of the lexical element with similar meanings in related languages and then use them to recover the archetype. And we don't have to think about from where the archetype came: it is well known that it was dreamt up arbitrarily by someone in ancient times. De Saussure's words sounded at the very beginning of the 20th century, "pregnant with revolutions". They came to be the battle cry for the cultural revolutions, which gave rise to a tradition of arbitrariness in painting, literature, graphic art and sculpture, teaching many to accept the artificial as art.

THE SMILE OF GOD
(the first signs and words)

The signs of the Sun that appeared in the Upper Palaeolithic (as archaeologists' findings tell us) were apparently the first complex graphemes of primitive writings. They were composed from two simple symbols - a Line (sometimes stylised as a "spear" – ↑) and an Angle (both soft and sharp); Lines and Circles. These combinations can be divined in many later hieroglyphs, even those that are loaded with diacritical additions.

If this basic composition can be deciphered, we can draw consciously closer to the rudiments of universal scripture and understand the mechanism that lies behind word creation.

...Geneticists and archaeologists generally agree that Homo Sapiens appeared in the east of Equatorial Africa (Kenya) some 100-150,000 years ago.

This information alone is sufficient for culturologists, linguists and historians of scripture to uncover subjects of interest.

The first faith was **Moon worship** (at the Equator the Sun was more likely seen as a devil than a god).

The first geometric figures depicted by humans were a circle and a semi-circle - the phases of the Moon.

It is important to stress that only at the Equator does the Moon float across the black sea of the African sky like a boat ᴗ .

In northern Africa, this boat is lifted by a storm wave ᴜ, while in Europe it is altogether standing on its end:). A young moon on the Equator was seen as the smile of god. In the north this was a crooked smile, which could have influenced the attitudes to such a god, which was in any event considerably transformed in the colder regions.

If faith in the Moon had arisen in the northerly latitudes (which is impossible), the Bull would never have become the worldly hypostasis of the Moon, or the sacred animal. And the Moon would not have received its name: only at the Equator is the moon associated with the horns of the African Buffalo. Thus, for the first believers, the Moon was represented in the golden horns of the black Sacred Bull.

**The endoethnonym of the Bull,
heard by the priests of the first two tribes (mů-ů-ůŋ и bů-ů-ůŋ)
came to be the name for the sacred sign of the Bull.**[1]

So what makes this episode in prehistory so important for linguistics?

The initial stage in the development of languages was, without doubt, **onomatopaeic**. During this lengthy period, humans, who were distinguished from other creatures because of an artistic talent—an ability to copy and impersonate, mastering the endoethnonyms of the "speaking" animals—developed their own organs of articulation which at first could only reproduce a limited combination of sounds, to reflect the immediate world around them. Here, however, mastering the endoethnonyms of other species, our primogenitors learned how to growl, hiss, quack, grunt, hoot, clang, squawk, cuckoo, crow, bleat, miaow and moo… **In other words, humans created their first words by giving names to other animals.**

Moon worship originated at this time and priests learned to depict a symbol of divinity that became the emblem and the charm of the first tribes. For the first time a name was given not to a speaking, but to a silent object, outwardly akin to a sign that already bore a name.

⌣ – *můŋ (*bůŋ) – 1) *Bull;* 2) *Moon, Luna.*

This name was then applied to different phases of the moon, including *full moon* (a circle).

In time the materials and tools for writing determined the *gothic* form of a variation of the sacred sign:

∨ – *můŋ (*bůŋ) – with the very same meanings.

This period in the history of language can be defined as **onomatopaeic**.

And it was to last until the time of the alphabetic script, which "officially" dates to the very end of the second millennium before the Common Era, when the Phoenician alphabet first appeared.

More than 90% of the words of all languages of humanity back then appeared befire the appearance of an alphabet. The figures are as approximate as the very age of Homo Sapiens, so we can replace them with the more accurate definition of the "absolute majority".

---

[1]*Yazyk Pisma*, Almaty-Rome, 1998, published by San Paolo, Stigraf Printing House, pp. 48-53. Republished in Collected Works, Almaty, published by Atamura Printing House, Vol. 4, pp. 54-60

PRIESTS

What can this status give linguistics?

The answer is a genuine foundation - an understanding that almost every word in any language (that arose before the second millennium before the Common Era) was at first **the name of a figurative graphic sign**. Therefore, to understand the genesis of the word, the form of the grapheme should be recovered, which was capable of giving rise to a lexical meaning, transforming the name of a sign into a conceptual word.

The mechanism for making a word:

Sign + name of sign + interpretation of sign = conceptual word

---

Example one:

ᴗ – ***mǔŋ (*bǔŋ)** – 1) *Horn;* 2) *Moon, Luna.* A variation of the symbol: **V**

The priests explained and interpreted the sign. The meanings of the words depended upon their imagination, knowledge and the sophistication of associated thought.

…When humans spread in number across the world, the moon was to change its position in the northern latitudes and, accordingly, so did its graphic image:

) > – the names by this time were also to change for phonetic reasons and one of the first meanings *(bull)* was to be lost.

Further, the old, still African signs, retaining their form, were to lose their meaning, *luna [moon]* and *mesyats [month]*, and the priests were forced to transfer their names (remaining from ***mǔŋ/*bǔŋ**) to items and phenomena that were outwardly similar to the signs.

Example.

In different, pra-Slavonic dialects for example, variations of a sign would be considered under the common name of **lǔŋ**, which would one day reach the Latin dictionary as **luna**, from where it would enter the later Slavonic languages.[2]

For now, though (still in Africa):

$$\cup \vee - *l\mathring{u}\eta - l\mathring{u}nq \begin{cases} l\mathring{u}nh \\ l\mathring{u}nkh - luna \\ l\mathring{u}nk \end{cases}$$

In the Slavonic dialects the nasal before another consonant would be systematically lost:

∪ ∨ – **log (lug), lok (luk), lokh (lůkh)**

From these signs of the *southern moon*, no longer recognised in the north, came many words in several tribes, using the forms and meanings of which a number of grammar rules can be recovered, which the *1001 Words* Universal Etymological Dictionary will cover in more detail.

Language is a collection of dialects. The Russian language has gathered words that have been derived from variations of a sign in different dialects, at different times and in different regions:

∪ – **log [ravine]** (*loge* [*couch*], *lozhka* [*spoon*], *lodka* [*boat*]), **lug [meadow]** (*лужа* [*puddle*]), **luk [onion]** (*luka* [*archer's bow*]

loza [cane, switch], lyzha [ski] (*lyzhva* [*a flat-bottom barge*]). And so on, with the vowel ending coming secondary.

---

[2] It is easier for me to present examples from Slavonic or Turkic languages, which in no way indicates that they are the most ancient. Examples that are equally as definitive can be found in many other dialects.

Culturologists would see the importance of the hieroglyph of the former sign for *Faith* becoming the symbol of *Untruth* (*falsehood*). From here we obtain figurative meanings, such as **loz**h [*a lie, falsehood*] (*l'gat* [*to lie*]) and ***lukavstvo*** [untruth, cunning].

This is now a direct echoing of Sun worship, which came in place of the previous religion. It is when the sign of the Moon is recognised as a symbol that is hostile to the true faith.

A softer attitude was formed with regard to the acute-angle variation of the sign, in dialect, where the compound bull vowel *ů was made as a simple labial *u.

v– **luk.** The priest saw the first manifestations of the rising sun in this sign **luk-i** – *luch* [*ray*], *luchshe* [*better*] etc.

In a different generation, another priest had transposed the name of the sign to the edible plant with straight, ray-like leaves – ***luk*** [***onion***]. (These two examples express the two rules of sign-based word creation, which will be discussed later).

As a counter to this, etymologists can be quoted articles from the best Etymological Dictionary of the Russian Language by Max Fasmer, which summarises the achievements of Slavicists over a century and a half of etymological research . Academic examples take up a lot of space, but they only add knowledge of the uppermost strata of the history of these words (about their prevalence in related and neighbouring languages and about attempts to recreate the *archetype*). However, not one article mentions anything about the genuine archetype of all these words (*lůŋ) or of its origin. In other words, that this lexeme was the name of a graphic sign. Without this the phonetic method does not allow one to penetrate deeper than the upper strata. Without it, not one of the words we have indicated (*log, lozh, loge, loza, lyzha, lug, luzha, luk* and so on) can be recognised as close relatives.

Real etymology begins when the meaning of a graphic sign and the associative imagination of the interpreter is recognised in the genesis of a word.

---

[3] Max Fasmer Etymological Dictionary of the Russian Language, M. 1967, M. 2009, vol. II, pp. 509-540.

THE FIRST RULE

The presented example already reflects the grammar rules of the language of the onomatopoeic period.

Rule 1 (R-1):

> **The name of a Sign is transferred to an item or phenomenon that is similar to it.**

∪ – 1) **log** – *a narrow, a hollow in a relief, a valley, a ravine;* 2) **lug** – *a hollow, a meadow.* ∨ – **luk [onion]** – *a plant with straight, ray-like leaves.* With time many other items that have received the name of signs have been assimilated to these signs. The number of homonyms would increase. This is perhaps the reason for the advent of **Rule II (R-2):**

> **The name of a Sign is transferred to an item or phenomenon that is similar to it in diminutive form.**

It is likely that the rule first arrived in culture, where this sign still preserved its vestiges of the sacred and its earlier semantics. Therefore, items similar to the sign for the Moon had to use its name in diminutive form: ∨ – **luk > luk-i > luči >** *luch* [*ray*].

This picture clearly demonstrates a sign with a later name: ∪ **lun(a)** – the Russian diminutive **lunka** – *an indent or hole in the soil.*

(Examples of the effect of this rule can be found in many languages. For example, ∪ – **aj** – *moon* > **ajak** – *bowl* (Turkic). The diminutive suffix in Ancient Turkic languages was-*ak*).

The very first formant of the diminutive in early language was the name for a spear – ***ha > a > wa**… Later, the formant ***j** (*arrow*) was added to it.

In Slavonic dialects, the application of both was reflected: **luka = *luk-i > luči > luč, *logi > lož'.**

The forms **lug-i > *luž', *log-i > lož'** turned up in dialects, where a more traditional formant was prominent, while the borrowed lexemes were corrected – **luža, loža (lože), ložka (lodka), lyža (lyžwa)...**

And only when the Moon finally lost its divinity in the culture of the Sun worshippers, the nocturnal celestial body was named in one of the non-Slav dialects according to Rule II, as a regular phenomenon, using the diminutive formant: ⌣ – **luŋ > luŋa > ... > luna.**

THE GRAMMAR OF THE NEGATIVE

With the movement away from the Equator to colder latitudes, the attitude of humans to the celestial bodies underwent significant changes. During cold nights they no longer enjoyed the moon's radiance, looking forward to the advent of the warm light. It was during the autumn and winter days and nights on the northern coast of the Mediterranean Sea that Sun worship was born. (Evidence of the place and time of the birth can be found in characteristic signs and idols of the sun worshippers in the Palaeolithic caves of Spain and France.)

The priests charged with creating signs were faced with a serious task: the creation of a graphic image of a new divinity, a new charm, to ensure that it was categorically nothing like the lunar charm of before. The priests rose to this challenge and they created signs of the Sun for their ethnoses, which expressed not an outward, credible appearance, but one common idea – **the negation of the sign for the Moon.**

We gained hieroglyphs, created considerably later than the first signs of the Sun, but they continued this same grammar of negation of the Moon. So is it from this time that everything new grows on the basis of negation of the past? This psychology appears in all fields of social life, in religion, in politics and in art. The phenomenon of negation came to be a natural factor in the process of development.

Forms of negation were approved and recognised in the era of Sun worship during a time of categorical negation of the Moon and all things lunar. The very first form of negation, the overturning, was formed back in the previous time, when the priests joined together the beginning and the end of the lunar cycle and expressed this opposition in the graphic:

⌣ – *young moon > the start of life, youth.*
⌢ – *old moon > the end of life, death.*

Anti-signs, created by turning over a hieroglyph (the name changed its shape and its meaning in the process), reached us in many different vocabularies. The ornaments still encounter similar, mirrored compositions: ⌣ ⌢, ↺, ∨ ∧, ⩔, ⊃⊂, ∂, ⇃ and so on.
Smile and Grief, Joy and Sadness, Life and Death all express these combinations of the young moon and the old moon.[4]

However the second meaning *(Bull)* pointed to a parallel solution: ⌣ Bull – ⌢ Cow (a Pollard or a Hump-backed animal). In the onomatopoeic age, too, when the first meanings had been forgotten but the names still remained the same, they acquired such meanings as ⌣ *yama* [*pit*] – ⌢ *holm* [*mound*] (burial), *gora* [*hill*] and so on.

We encounter negation through overturning in pictures that date back tens of thousands of years. These are subjects from Palaeolithic caves. A live deer is depicted on its feet; a dead deer, flipped over by 180° with all four legs pointing upward. Or with a spear in its side.

---

[4] One of the earliest oppositions of the symbol and the name was preserved in Turkic-Oghuz: ⌣ ol – *live, be;* ⌢ öl – *die*. I will relate more about this pair which, it seems, also became wi despread in Africa, a little later.

A SPEAR IN THE SIDE - A SIGN OF NEGATION

The second and most fundamental form of negation of the Moon in scripture in the age of Sun worship was the combination of signs of the Moon (ᴗ V) ˃ O) with a spear (Ψ ᵾ ᵥ ∀ D ≽ Q Q), with a stone (ᴗ V ꙅ ≽ ◉) or with a *wound* from a spear (ᴗ ∀ ꙅ ≽ ◉). In Ancient Egypt, a *wound* on the body of the Moon was depicted with red paint.

When the archer's bow was invented, the wounding of the Moon was ascribed to an arrow in a number of cultures. Its name *j was to compete with the more ancient name for a spear *ha.

Before the fourth, third and second millennia, forms of a spotted sun came from ancient Palaeolithic times – ⊙ ra (Ancient Egypt). ⊙ –*sun* (Ancient Chinese), unknown name. D jaj – sun (Ancient Turkic), ≽ ud – *sun* (Sumerian) and ⊟ ři – *sun* (Chinese).

The forms of these signs and the origin of their names are all explained in *1001 Words*. They all express this first idea - the negation of the Moon. In Egyptian and Ancient Chinese, the key element in a compound sign is the *Full Moon*. In Ancient Turkic and Sumerian is the *Northern Moon* ( ) ≽).

Right here, on this page, we can perform an etymological analysis of an Ancient Turkic hieroglyph and its name:

D **jaj** – 1) *sun;* 2) *onion* (Ancient Turkic)

) **aj** – *luna, moon* (Ancient Turkic)

I ***j** – **arrow* (universal)

This analysis reveals Rule III, the Rule of the Compound Sign (R-3):

If you combine signs, combine their names, too

𐰑 𐰑 *j – aj > jaj

According to this Rule, the most ancient compound signs were created. And this rule remained in place right until the end of the age of the figurative script.

However, this method was used to name the signs of the Sun in Ancient Turkic and Sumerian. (It was not the same in Ancient Egypt.)

NEGATION – DIMINUTION

Having mastered the grammar of negation when creating the first compound hieroglyphs and their names, priests handed down these rules over thousands of generations with the emblems and charms they were bequeathed along the way. The same set of signs was used, enriched with new functions and nuances in their meanings.

For example, ↻ Ψ. The spear *****ha** or, later, the arrow *****j** was seen in one culture as a total negation of the Horns (Bull) and the compound sign was given the name Pollard – Cow *(because the females of the wild horned cattle had no horns). Thus, the functional word **-a, -j** formed the antonym.

In another culture, the priest saw that the spear/arrow merely halves, or diminishes the horns. Here the sign designated Little Horns (Calf) or the little horned one (Ram). In these languages, **-a, -j** – are a formant for diminution.

[Killing the Moon – they killed the Bull. Thus, in creating the sign of the Sun, they created signs of the Non-Bull – Cow, Ram, Calf, Ox... Humans, it appears, became meat-eaters for real when worshipping the Sun - the fire. To become Sun worshippers, humans had to bring the Black Bull as a sacrifice for their new god.

The ritual of tauromachy, it seems, began in Spain and it was not to end there, by any means. But they killed the Bull, so as to give life to the hornless and small-horned animals that were acknowledged as the worldly representatives of the Sun. They had to be fed, cared for, protected from predators and not offered in sacrifice, either to the Moon or to the Sun. Hindus still abide by this tradition, holding the cow in high esteem and not eating any meat. The priests of the other [new] religions could not get to the bottom of the grammar of negation and they began offering the Ram in sacrifice. They were happy to use the the cow and the calf, too].

Negation (and not diminution) became the main grammar of the languages that formed by the third millennium before the Common Era, which bears witness to the earlier spread of the meaning of negation. External and internal inflexions (a, j), negating a name, create a verb; negating a verb, they form a name; negating the singular, they create the plural, and so on. 1001 Words covers this in more detail.

THE SECOND OUTCOME

...All languages that formed by the third millennium before the Common Era arose in the Ancient World. This means Africa (the period of moon worshipping), the Mediterranean, Asia Minor, Ancient Western Asia (the Tigris and the Euphrates). The ethnoses, still small numbers of humans, were in fairly close contact with one another and cultural exchanges provided for all the similarities that we encounter and will encounter yet further in the languages and writings of the ancient peoples, spread over the course of history to all corners of the Eurasian supercontinent and beyond, to the Polynesian Islands and to America.

Five thousand years ago saw the start of the migration of peoples from the countries of the Ancient World to the East. They were led there in the search for the homeland of the Sun by the Young Sun cult, which arose because of an error in the interpretation of the Egyptian sign ☉ **Ra** with a red dot. Not all peoples carried the Egyptian sign to the ends of the earth, retaining the colour of the spot. But the Japanese succeeded.

All peoples of the East, the Far East, Southeast Asia, Polynesia and the Americas came to their current lands relatively recently. Archaeologists confirm that the earliest cultural monuments of Central Asia and further east are no older than from the third to the second millennium before the Common Era. In the European part of Eurasia, though, monuments from the seventh millennium before the Common Era can be observed. The concepts of civilisation, such as stick farming, the smelting of gold, tin, copper, bronze, iron and others came to the countries of the Rising Sun from the western part of Eurasia. The same can be said for the rudiments of the languages and scriptures of the East.

This all speaks of the genetic and cultural relationship of peoples who headed East in search of the Home of the Sun and of those whose priests who would not believe in this cult, and the ethnoses remained within the territories of the Ancient World.

FURTHER TO THE ABOVE

The history of languages is the history of scripture. And these closely related elements of culture can no longer be considered separately. From early times, humans have adapted to relay and receive information not only verbally, but graphically as well, reading tracks in wet soil and, later, by scratching signs that speak.

It is likely that the **onomatopoeic** period, too, would not have got by without such writings.

The onomatopoeic period can logically be divided into two sub-periods. **The Early Scripture period**, when the graphic symbol strove to be naturalistically figurative. And the **Scripture period**, where the graphic sign lost its naturalistic figurativeness.

1) It strove to express not only the outward similarity to an item or a phenomenon, but the ideology of the symbol in question. This is a hieroglyph.
2) The sign was to express the syllabic or phonemic sound. This is the syllabic and literal word.

APPROACHES TO THE *1001 WORDS* DICTIONARY

To verify the version of interdependence of the Graphic Sign and the Word, we only have to look at a number of graphemes from hieroglyphic systems - Sumerian, Ancient Egyptian and Ancient Chinese. Primarily these are signs of the Sun and their different names. To do this, however, we have to recover one more rule from the First Grammar.

RULE IV (R-4):

> If a compound sign is adopted, but its name cannot be broken down into component parts, to give the item a name we have to negate the overall name of the compound sign.

...The principal sign for Ancient Egypt was ☉ **Ra** – 1) *sun;* 2) *god of the Sun* (third to second millennium before the Common Era). All ethnoses living at that time in the Mediterranean were probably familiar with it. The Slavs found themselves there, too. The red spot had to be given a name. **Ra** cannot be broken down into component parts. Thus, Rule IV is applied: ***Ra-no > rano** – *morning* (Czech), **ranok** – *morning* (Ukr.). In Russian two forms with negating suffixes, **no** and **ni**, remain: **rano** – *early*, **ran'** – *the early hour.*

In a tribe where the red spot was still not adopted as the young sun, this item was conceived traditionally, as it was expressed in the semantics of the word ***ra-na > rana** – *wound.*

Based on the meaning of the word, the form of the sign can be recovered. In one Slavic tribe the materialised sign for the sun as *The Moon with a Wound* was a stone or wooden disc with a hole in the middle. The hole in this dialect was named using a prepositional negation: ***no-Ra > nora** – *hole, burrow.*

The Slavs saw the sign **Ra** in different forms: with a red spot and with a hole and this found its reflection in the word.

(In the dialect that used the negation **di-** the name of a hole appeared in the sign ***di-Ra**. The Slavonic languages now had **dyra** – *hole.*)

THE FIFTH RULE

☉ – **Ra**. Central detail: **Ra- no.**

(the name appears in Slavonic and Persian languages)

The negating formant is nowadays applied only in prepositional form: **na, no, ne-**. The *Dictionary* will consider many Slavonic examples with the obsolete **-no, -n**. Such a situation with postfix and prefix (prepositional) application of the negating formant is, I hope, recoverable in Persian dialects and dialects, too.

The word **ranó** means 1) *young*, and 2) *wonderful* (Persian). It would appear that these are the first figurative meanings from the very first – *morning sun*. The rousing feature of the sun worshipping priest. In the Slavonic languages, a word formed by a negation received no figurative meanings. It was the Persians who worked on the language more meticulously. They applied **Rule V (R-5):**

> **By negating the name of the Detail of a compound sign, you obtain the name of another Detail.**

The Persians had to learn the name of the basic detail – the circle, which was perceived as the opposite of the wonderful red spot. At that time it used the prepositional negation *j: ***j-Rano >*j-ran**

At first it is probable that the meaning they had in mind was the opposite of the young sun, meaning either *old sun* or another "nickname", perhaps, for the Moon? Time would pass, though, and whole settlements and cities would be built based on the design of the Egyptian sign for the Sun. "Built", having in mind here "the god's standpoint": the Sun, looking down from above, should see its sign, so as to guard over its true believers. Based on this plan, architects created city states and this sign gradually became the plan for nation states and then for the entire world, in the centre of which each ethnos, without parting with this divine sign, could see itself for thousands of years.

◉ – The formula of ethnocentrism. (Also expressing egocentrism.)

In one of these ethnoses, when the Point, long since no longer red and, therefore, having lost its first name, needed a new one. And it was obtained, once again, using the Fifth Rule, because the name of the main Detail (the circle) was already known – ***j-ran(o)**. It became the name of a country, the symbolic borders of which were designated by a spacious circle.

And it is probable that at this point the Sumerian and Persian name for an arrow was used: **ti, til, tir** – *arrow* (Sumerian) **tihr** – *arrow* (Persian)

Hypothesis: ***tihr-jran, *ti-jran**. This combination of words may have given rise to several compound words – a) tihr- ran, b) tirran, c) tiran and others.

When etymologists set about ascertaining the origin of the Persian title Tigran, the name of the city Tehran and the Latin-Greek **tyrannus** – *tyrant, almighty ruler* (as they say in certain quarters), they should without fail have the sign of **Ra** before their eyes, imagine its history and concede that the Point at the centre, in different eras, could symbolise the capital of a nation, a great leader and then a people, elected by god (Tyrrhenians was what the Greeks called the Etruscans).

TRACES OF THE SIGN OF THE OX

...For the Introduction to the *1001 Words* Universal Etymological Dictionary all that is required are the Rules of the Grammar of Negation that have been recovered and an example from the youngest scriptures – Phoenician (the end of the second millennium before the Common Era). This alphabet was probably collated from the emblems and signs of the nomadic tribes of Asia Minor and Ancient Western Asia. At the end of a long war it was customary for a corresponding treaty of eternal brotherhood to be concluded and the leaders of the tribes carved out the symbols of their tribes on some prominent rock, as if placing their signatures to the treaty.

There were a good many such writings in the Great Steppe, too, from Altai to the Danube, but the centuries of Islam and Christianity showed no mercy to the pagan writings. Tribal signs are still preserved in the culture of the Kazakhs, yesterday's nomads. And these signs, both in outward appearance and in names, are the typical hieroglyphs that we encounter in the most ancient of systems. Emblems included into the Phoenician alphabet were most likely also hieroglyphs. The emblems of Indo-European and Semitic tribes. There were no longer any other ethnoses among them. By this time they had left Ancient Western Asia for the East. The signs of the *sun animals*—the Cow, Ram, Calf, Ox and Camel—came to be the emblems and charms of the sun worshippers... There were several of these gathered within the Phoenician alphabet. And it begins with the hieroglyphic letter ⌅ **'alef** – *ox* (Semitic).

This compound sign will help us recover another rule of the first grammar. Negation of the negation **(R-6).**

NEGATION OF THE NEGATION

We have seen that the negation method:

1) **was used to create antonyms:** the name of the Sun is the opposite (in meaning) of that of the Moon; the name of the Cow (Ram, Calf, Ox, Pollards) is the opposite of that of the Bull; in future the sign for Wife was obtained from the negation of the sign for husband and so on;

2) **was used to created grammatical opposites**: noun – verb; verb – name; nominative –genitive; singular – plural; masculine – feminine and so on.

By negating the overall name of the compound sign, they obtained the name of the detail (R-4).

By negating the name of the detail, they obtained another name (R-5).

This collection of Rules of the Grammar of Negation is more than enough to set about the familiar etymology. This means analysing the word that has a graphical sign. The vast majority of lexical elements have long since moved away from these signs. Therefore, the signs have to be reinstated. How is this done? Their forms are embedded in the meanings of words. Therefore it is simpler to begin with the existing names of graphical signs. Such signs were preserved in the first alphabet (Phoenician), the letters of which were in fact the proto-hieroglyphs. (Later hieroglyphs with phonetic and numerical additions were not accepted in the emblems.)

In later alphabets (in Cyrillic, for example) the letters have secondary names that are not related to the shape of the sign.

BOUSTROPHEDONIC LETTERS

◁ - *ox* (Phoenician)

There was probably another version in the variations of the Phoenician alphabet that did survive to our time. The Greeks probably saw it, which is why in certain monuments to Ancient Greek scripture we encounter not only the regular alpha A , but also the ▲..

It is this version that can hint at a possible precursor, which could have been the Sumerian hieroglyph ∀ **gud** – *bull*. It was probably not by chance that the Semites, having adopted the "horned head", altered its position in the graphical form. By placing it on its side they created an image of a *bull, but not quite.* By changing both the name and the meaning. It is possible that the Slavs also "placed the bull" on its side. The *bull laid down*, as the Russian peasants would call a castrated bull, becomes the ox. This then means that the grammaticians placed the Phoenician letter not on its feet, but on its horns ◁ – ▲

For the Greeks the former hieroglyph had lost all of its imagery: they saw neither a *bull* nor an *ox* in it. But still, why did the letter change its position?

The historian of scripture explains that this evolution of the sign is a feature of the cultural development of Greece of that time. This was expressed in a striving to give a harmony, to suit the tastes of the Hellene, even to graphical signs: "the Greeks somewhat altered the shape of the Phoenician letters. Without losing their affinity with the Phoenician, the Greek letters, in accordance with the traditions of architecture and ornamentation, acquired a more complete geometrical form. For example,

('alef) –   (alpha)."[5]

I see the main reason lying elsewhere. Having adopted the Phoenician script, the Greeks wrote from right to left. Such a direction of the line is attested in the most ancient of inscriptions.

Then the Greeks switched to a writing method that was given the name *boustrophedon*, from the Greek *bus (bull)* and *strophe (turn)*. With this method the first line follows from right to left, the second, from left to right, the third from right to left and so on, like the furrow behind a bull on a ploughed field. This method proved to be incredibly time-consuming for scholars: when changing the direction of the line, the writer would have to turn the letters, following in one direction, to follow the other. In the first instance - alpha. If at first it was ◄, , in the second line it was ►, in the third it was ◄ again and so on until the end of the text. I am sure that this is the main reason that forced the Greek authors of symbols to change the position both of the alpha and of a number of other letters. He focused attention on the letters that did not need to be turned: they would be written identically whatever direction the text would follow. There were several such letters in the Greek alphabet; **I** – jota, **T** – tau, **O** – o-miкron, **Ϙ** – fita, **M** – miu, **H** – eta.

The Greeks understood their advantage and they began creating similar equilaterals based on their kind, which now can confidently be called boustrophedonic letters.

Name	Letters	
	pre-Greek	boustrophedonic
alfa	◄	A A A
delta	◁	✻
mi	ᗯ	M
pe	⌐	Π
lambda	⌐	Λ

Of course, not all of them could be given an equilateral form. The letters gamma – **Γ**, kappa – **K**, po – **P** and epsilon – **E** cannot be made boutrophedonic. However, in the process of reconstructing five letters, the remaining ones, too (even those that are non-reversible), acquired a so-called "more complete geometrical appearance. In accordance with the traditions of Greek architecture and ornamentation".

---

[5] V.A. Istrin, *Vozniknoveniye i razvitiye pisma, Nauka,* Moscow, 1965, p. 339. Johannes Friedrich *Istoriya Pisma*. M. 1979 – did not touch on this matter. The same applies to Čestmír Loukotka's *Razvitie Pisma* M. 1950 and others

A FULL FIVE MARKS!

The first draft of *The Code of the Word* was read by a respected linguist from the Russian People's Friendship University Sergei Preobrazhensky, who wrote "The author does not believe that separate, acute considerations such as the influence of the boustrophedon on the central symmetry of Ancient Greek graphemes are worthy of long-winded discussion (a "professional" would regret it), but Olzhas Suleimenov, who is not afraid to dabble in guesswork, goes further in the search for connections and leaves the details to the discretion of the reader".

I have to admit that I would like to continue the discussion on the subject of *Boustrophedonic* letters that I began, and it would be of interest to talk about other features of the Phoenician-Greek letter-based relations, especially given that this cultural background is more familiar to the wider audience than the overly specific problems of figurative scripture, but I was afraid to veer away from the central theme. Getting distracted was an easy matter, too, as I know that the history of the Greeks developing the Phoenician alphabet is given incredibly scant attention and, I can assert that this has a restraining influence on European etymology. The reviewer's comment allows me to digress a little and touch upon the fate of yet another Phoenician letter in the Greek and Latin alphabets. This story will also be a short one, but I think it will be sufficiently informative as, like the boustrophedonic letters, it may spur an interested scholarly reader to delve deeper into these subjects.

So why did the name of the Phoenician letter ϙ kof, when the archi-Greeks adopted the alphabet, transform into ϟ (in the classic alphabet, fta, with the addition of the symbolic flex-ion –ta, as in beta, delta, jota, eta, zeta etc)? The phonetic nature of the transformation of k>ϟ cannot be proven.

Which of the historians of scripture asked themselves this question? Not Loukotka, not Istrin and not Friedrich. An "amateur" is given the option, though.

This one transformation of the name of the Phoenician letter places in doubt the accuracy of the scientifically asserted chart of the spread of the alphabet in the Mediterranean:
Phoenician>Greek>Etruscan>Latin.

The sequence proposed by the "professionals" is simply not possible:

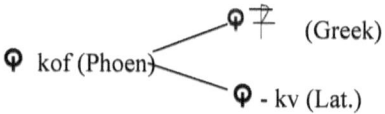

The schedule of the shift of the letter (and the alphabet?) appears more likely:

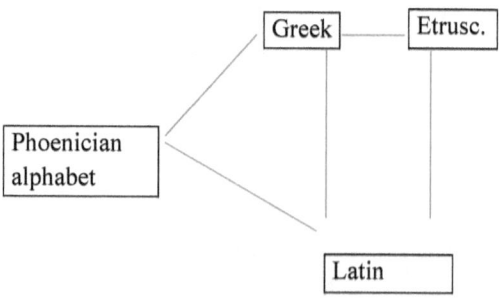

Therefore, it is now worth discussing the following version:

```
            ┌─────────┐──────┌────────┐
            │  Greek  │      │ Etrusc.│
            └─────────┘      └────────┘
┌──────────────┐   /                │
│  Phoenician  │  ∠                 │
│  alphabet    │                    │
└──────────────┘ \                  │
                  \                 │
                   \  ┌────────┐
                      │ Latin  │
                      └────────┘
```

Latin

The theory of families of languages speaks of the fact that the numerals of the first ten of them originated in the pre-languages. What this means is that all names for the number *five* in Indo-European languages stem from a common archetype. So how did this combination of sounds form? That is something we do not know. For now the statement is sufficient. Phonetics enables the Germanic ffe (English), fünf (German) to be hitched to this archetype. For Latin, however, and, accordingly, the Romantic languages, this is impossible: quinque (Latin) oral Ital-ian – kvinkve.

The presented forms speak more of the written than of the oral origin of the numeral. And not in the pre-languages, rather in the languages of separate ethnoses that assimilated the alpha-betic script. This written numeral most likely accompanied the numerical symbol such as the Latin V or the Ancient Greek ⌒ - *five*. Here we try to recover the table with the figure and the recovered name:

⌒ * ΦIN ΦE (Φ-I-N- Φ-E)

The Teutons read it "in the Greek way":

*f-i-n-f-e < ffe (анг.)
fünf (нем.)

The Romans read it "in the Latin way":

*kv-i-n-kv-e > quinque

This reading enables us to determine the etymological passport of the word, with its date of birth and "nationality": the middle of the first century BCE, the Mediterranean, where the Greek and Latin alphabets vied with one another. Now, though, we are not clarifying the deepest stratum in the history of the word. This is covered in the Universal (meaning multinational) ety-mological dictionary *1001 Words*.

The Code of the Word has been written to engage linguists from all over the world to work on the dictionary, as clarifying the genesis of the First Words of the First Language is a matter for eve-ryone. The Internet will help to bring together a union of like thinkers.

But how did we get ko ₽>₽ ?

Here the etymologist would find knowledge of the <u>false article</u>, still an unknown subject in linguistics, to be of great use. Some examples: the Turkic words beginning with a syllable that is similar to Slavonic articles, when they entered the Slavonic languages, underwent a re-structuring. For example, <u>toprakh</u> – *dust (*Ancient Turkic) >*<u>to prakh</u> – *prakh [ash], pyl' [dust], porokh [gunpowder], poroshok [powder]*. <u>Tostakan</u> – *chasha [cup] (Chagat.)* >*<u>to stakan</u> - stakan (glass, tumbler]* (Ancient Russian). <u>Togay</u> – *roshcha [grove], lesok [wood]* > <u>to gay</u> – *gai – roshcha* (Ancient Russian, Ukrainian) and so on.

If this subject were to be checked in other languages as well, we could concede that the Greeks, when borrowing the Phoenician name kof, they erroneously heard their own indefinite article o(*ho).

And the restructuring of hof >* ho ƿ took place.
This etymology brings us closer to an understanding of the origins of the true archetype of the name of the number *five*.

In *1001 Words* the family tree of the letter ϙ ko ƿ. will be traced in detail which, before it appeared in the Phoenician alphabet, spent time in a number of proto-hieroglyphic scriptures (which have not survived to this day) in the role of the symbol for Cow Ψ ko ƿ (kow, kov) and was best preserved in this form in Aramaic ϙ ko ƿ.

The ideology of the compound sign of the slain Bull (non-Bull) was expressed as a combina-tion of simple elements – Horn (u), Spear (ha). It unfolfed in language in such a way that the sub-ordinate symbol was read first. (The name of the compound symbol was preserved in the word *kow – cow* (Arm.), *kov – cow* (Engl.), qou, qō – ditto (Ind.).

In other ancient-European languages the compound symbol for *Slain Bull* was probably used in tribes of hunters as a sign for a Catch, or a Possession. In any case we should call on this re-covered hieroglyph when studying the etymology of the Italian verb ho (*I have*) (*haŭ >*hō) and the roots of the Latin verb *havere,* the German haben and the English *have.*

In Ancient Chinese, there is the hieroglyph Ψ - *cow*. The name has not yet been recovered, but I believe it is connected with the contemporary *niu - cow* (*j-u > *ŋj-u). The symbol very clearly expresses the ideology of *Slain Bull > Non-Bull.*

The Chinese took another, albeit unrecognised, version of the sign of the cow with them to the East, in which the spear is positioned horizontally, but which is interpreted differently: ⌣ mouth. I think that the grammatician saw the lower part of the face and the line of the mouth here.

He then created a secondary structure ⱴ tongue, ⱴ and sound. The name of the hieroglyph today is ▭ *kou* (*mouth*).

I believe that the parallels with the name of the sign for the Cow, which went as far as the Phoenician alphabet, and with the words *kow, kov, qō - cow* (Indo-European) enable us to assume that in the Ancient Chinese, too, the hieroglyph for *mouth* (*cow) was named the same way that it is named today.

...However, we will end our digression from the main theme there and return to the travels of the sign of that other *Non-Bull*, the Ox.

ALPHA
(novellas)

In the middle of the first millennium before the Common Era, the Europeans identified the first letter when familiarising themselves with the Greek alphabet. This is perhaps because it was the most figurative of all the rest. It must have been especially to the liking of the residents of the mountainous parts of Europe: in it they saw an image of mountain peaks, atop which the snow does not melt even in the summer. They probably named these mountains with the name of this sign ⋀ ⋀ **alfa** > **alpa.*

Its upper part (the scalp), according to the Fourth Rule (*negate the overall name to name the Part*) was given its name, having applied the method of negating the negation. This could have taken place in the adverb, where the negation was implemented with the postfix -a. Then part of the name left *[to the snowy part of the sign]*: ***alf.** Is this not how the Latin root **albus** – *white* (-us – masculine, suffix, adjective) arose?

...There were other interpretations as well: ⋀ - *legs* (we recall that Egypt was next door, in the writings of which there was such a hieroglyph ⋀, probably also familiar to the surrounding cultures). Such an association may have prompted the priest to conclude, in interpreting the alpha, that: ⋀ – *short legs > small man.*

Here the Germanic **elf** – *dwarf* comes to mind (***'alef** > **elef** – a regressive assimilation of the quality of the sound in Germanic, manifested especially in the German language). And ancient Indian – 'alpa – 1) *small, short* 2) a *few, littleness.*

By removing a part (the horizontal dash of the negation), the affix is removed, applying the rule of negation of the negation: ∧ **alp** – *giant* (Turkic)

...In Spain, to the south of Valencia is the small town of Calpe. The place differs from all other towns on the coastline in one respect - some one hundred metres from the beach a tall, sharp-pointed rock protrudes from the water. The rock, protruding from the water, is like a sign ∧ **'alfa** – there is both a sharp-pointed part above the water and an underwater base. The Greek name of the sign was clearly pronounced by Semites, who have not lost the earlier guttural sound, as was made by the Greeks and others. These parts of Spain were inhabited by Arabs in the Middle Ages.

...On the southern coast of the Mediterranean, the sign of the Ox was pronounced here with an already Greek vowel ending, which appeared by no means to negate the meaning, rather to open the final syllable: **'alef – alfa, bet – beta, jot – jota, het** – heta and so on. At the same time it retained is earlier position of lying on its side. And the rounded consonant was coarsened. Based on the "design" of the sign, a musical instrument was created ◀ · – **'arfa** - *harp*. It is quite possible that the hieroglyphic meaning was preserved here too: musical instruments in the shape of heads with horns were made in Ancient Egypt. So was this in honour of the Sun? After all, crossed-out horns mean not only the Cow or the Ox, but also the negated Moon.

The Semites could have pronounced the sign *Alpha* as *Carfa*. Carthage must be destroyed! The follies of associated thought. A traveller was brought to the king of this region (now Tunis). "For what are you asking?" "A little land, that is all." "How much?" "My ox fell dead on my journey. I removed its hide. I would like a piece of land that is no bigger than his hide." The king laughed and permitted the traveller to measure out a piece of land with his hide. The man cut the hide into thin, rope-like strips, tied them together and measured out an entire city, which he called Carthage and populated with his nomadic race: **genus** – *race* (Latin).[6]

What better time to recall a number of words from the English dictionary, too. I would try to apply this sign in its different positions:

◄ – 'alef >... > **calf**

A – 'alef >... > **half**

The words arose in different dialects and at different times. The first when the sign was still a full-fledged hieroglyph. This is evidenced in the meaning of the word.

---

[6] It is quite possible that the start of the word is related to the literal *carve* – *ox*, Polish dialect *karw* – *ox*. And the Slavonic name for cow *carva* > *krava* (Czech, Slovenian, Serbo-Croat, Bulgarian, Slovak)

AS FAR BACK AS IN SUMER?

The fact that the ancestors of the English encountered this hieroglyph in Ancient Western Asia may be imparted in the subject of the following novella.

... ◁ – 'alef > *elev (regressive assimilation of vowel quality in Germanic languages).

▷ – elev – in

A turn of 180° – negation. The negating formant – **in, -n**, observed in ancient languages, is added to the name. (In Latin there is already the prepositional negation **in-, ni-** .) In all languages that have been touched by Sumerian influence there are words in which the Sumerian harmony of vowels has left a clear trace; the first vowel of the word assimilates the next. If the first vowel is e, the subsequent vowels will be, too: ***elev-in** > **eleven** In Sumerian ▷ – *ten* | – *unit*. Such a compound figure was yet to be encountered in Sumerian monuments. However it really could have been. Subsequent generations of proto-Britons, analysing the compound numeral, separated **elev** from it, deciding that this was *ten*, while the negating formant was taken as **one**. Especially given that the Sumerian harmony of vowels would still have evened out the vowels.

Then they risked creating another number:

▷ – **eleven – 11**
▶ – ***tu – elev > twelve – 12**

There was not enough space for a third unit.

These exploratory examples are tied into the forms of a specific sign and, therefore, words that arise from its name gain a kind of etymological passport that tells us of their genesis, time and regions of origin. And how they were made. In an ideal scenario, every word should obtain such a passport. Then we could speak of total etymology.

HOW TO TURN OX INTO LION

We have learnt that the Phoenician Ox left its tracks in the African coast of the Mediterranean Sea (Carthage, harp) but, it would appear, it also spent time in Central Africa, where the principal representatives of African fauna are to be encountered. Words derived using this same Sign tell us this. They inform us of when the Teutons, the Slavs, Latin speakers and the Greeks first visited the depths of Africa and where they saw animals that are not found either in Europe or in Asia. No reports remain of expeditions by the ancient Europeans in any written monument, yet the word 'alef has preserved this sensational information. And they are revealed if we continue studying it together with the sign.

◄ – **'alef** – *ox* (Phoenician)

If we analyse the compound sign and remove the *spear* of negation, the negating preposition then leaves: – ***lef > *lew**

The priest saw the open mouth of the king of the animals. Only in Slavonic languages does a lexical element remain that is closest to the archetype.

The Latin **leō** – *lion* is phonetically more remote. And in some ancient Germanic language the syllable is enclosed by a prosthetic nasal consonant: ***leon** – *lion*. But it is found in Greek.

Fasmer believes that the Latin **leō** gave rise to the Old High German **lëwo** – *lion*, while the Slavs were to adopt this term from the Teutons and shed the superfluous vowel ending: ***lëw(o)** – **lev** (F., vol. II p. 471).

HCC (historical and cultural considerations) – the ideological basis of modern etymology. The etymological chain of Latin > Ancient Germanic > Slavonic is in agreement with HCC. (*All roads of the word lead from Rome*)

There are questions, however, which this version is unable to answer. For example, the Slavs would not have done away with the vowel at the end of the word. If it had been at the beginning then, yes, this would have been possible. This is because the Slavonic languages, especially in the Eastern Slavonic languages, which preserved more from the pre-Slavonic, contain a powerful inertia of the open syllable. Therefore, by adopting lexical elements with a consonant at the end, in enunciatory practice, they were adding a prosthetic vowel at the end of the word. And if the Slavs really had adopted **lëwo**, it would not have lost the vowel from the end.

WHERE DID THE OX GO?

The Slav priest, only now probably in different times and in different regions, continued to work with the obtained sign of the Lion, not altering its direction. He added the horizontal line -*j:

< —*lev-j *left*

Perhaps this explains the origin of the word *levj – *left* (Bulg. – левы, Ukr. – лівий, Czech. – levy, Slovak. – l'avj, Pol. – lewy).

The pointer of the direction to the left in another dialect gets by without adding the horizontal line, which is from where the corresponding name arrives:

< *lev – *left* (the meaning of main predator was probably already forgotten). The word in such a form is widespread in a number of Slavonic languages: Old Slavonic левъ – *left*, Bulg. – ляв, Sloven. – lev.

The sign was imbedded in the meaning of the Latin laevus – *left, arched.*

Dictionaries find no matches to the Slavonic word in other languages. Although poets, knowing of the root rhyme, would have called upon the English **left** for comparison.

[*The ending is reminiscent of the alternation of j/d (t), not noted by the Indoeuropeans, which was manifested, perhaps, only in the Turkic languages. (There are many examples. Here are just the most evident: **uj** – cow (Kirg.), **ud** (Khak.), **ut** – ditto (Alt.) In Ancient Turkic texts: **ajak = adak, atak** – leg; **kajyn= kadyn, katyn** – wife, spouse etc).*

If linguists and specialists in Germanic studies in particular knew that many phenomena in languages, diluted over different families, had a common origin, they would have found instance of such alternation in the languages they were studying. They would have found an explanation for the difference and the similarity of the English you (obs. *ju) and the German du. They would have seen the correspondence between the German ja! and the Russian да! (In Russian, related words рой and род [brood and breed], **стая** (staja – flock) and **стадо** (*stada – herd) have been collected from different dialects. This alternation is a subject for an excellent dissertation. It explains the link between this alternation and processes that took place in ancient writings. In particular, it explains what could unite the Latin **D** and Ancient Turkic **D** – j.

Why is the soft Cyrillic **Щ** in Russian writing called *šia*, but in Bulgarian it is *šta*.

And all these examples lead to the conclusion that the name of the sign for arrow in universal scripture (Line) developed phonetically in a multitude of dialects under a provisional scheme: *j - 'j - dži - di(ti) - d(t).

And the sign **I** (or **—**) in different scriptures was called simply *j*, or *di*, or *d(t)*. So, therefore, uj – cow and ut – cow in neighbouring languages is the result not of the verbal alternation of sounds, but of a written alternation. And the Bulgarian shta – **Щ** came from sha – **Ш**, because the softening line (going downwards) was seen by a Bulgarian grammatician as *t*, while the Russian-speakers read it as *i*.

It is from such "minor details" that the marked role of the Line (Negation (Reduction, Increase, Softening) is formed in the grammar of the Sign and the Word. However, we can also judge to what extent it has not been noticed by science by the fact that the Slavonic numeral odin (edin – one) stands alone among the Indoeuropean numerals. Now, though, we can compare the western Slavonic – e-di-n with the German ***e-j-n*** – one. In the archetype it is nearer to the Easterm Slavonic ***o-di-n***, which, perhaps, rises to the hypothetical ***o-j-n***. Which is realised in the Ancient Latin oin – один – one! This is not by chance: it is supported by the Irish **oin** – one.

...The German ein arose thanks to the regressive assimilation of the quality: ***oin > ein***. In written form the assimilated form is retained while, in the verbal, that which is nearer to the initial version came out on top (***ojn > ajn***).

*In western Slavonic **edin** felt the influence of the Germanic regressive assimilation of the sound quality. The same with the Polish **krev** – blood, which came from **krov'**.*

*The subject of alternation is a fascinating one, but we shall stop at the comparison of the English **J am** (obs. ***aj am**?) and the Ancient Persian **Ad am** – I am.*

*It is possible that this is how the Turkic **adam** – man, comes from and the name of the first man from Bible legend who announced himself to the whole world with his name **Adam** – I am!*]

In summary, I assume that the Slavonic ***lev-j** and the English **lef-t** – are names from one sign, which came to be not in Africa (which could be evident from the loss of the first meaning of the main element **lef = lev**), but at the same time and, possibly, in one region.

Thus:

< **lef = lev**

<− **lef-t = lev-j** – *to the left, left.*

(In the scripture of that time, the meanings of the ancillary sign (the line) could have differed. The vertical line (spear) **-a** was a negation; the horizontal line (*arrow*) **-j** – not a negation.) We can assume that the variations of the line in the writings of the ethnoses (that derived these words) also performed syntactical functions. Russian contains the most expressive of their traces:

a – alternative conjunction (*negation*),

i – coordinating conjunction (*increase*).

In certain other Slavonic languages only one name of the Line has remained in both meanings. For example, the Czech **a** (both a coordinating conjunction and a negating preposition).

THE OX GIVES RISE TO THE ELEPHANT?

The Teutons, too, could have been on that expedition into deepest Africa, because only in the Germanic **'alef** can we experience the regressive assimilation of the sound quality.

◄ – 'alef > elef

A change in the initial vowel influenced the subsequent rebuilding of the word, when the sign was relieved of the negating element (the line). The initial vowel was no longer even reminiscent of the negating preposition **a-**. Therefore, they had to resort to another formant with a similar function.

< – *elef -anti

Judging by the meaning obtained, the interpreter of the sign saw in this instance not the mouth of the king of the predators but the tusks of the emperor of the herbivores. The pre-Germanic name **elefant** then entered Latin as **elefantus** – *elephant.*

The word **anti** was widespread in western languages to denote the *opposite.* (From the Greek it entered the Russian: **Antichrist.** Many neologisms have been formed according to this model. In Latin, **anti** – *ancient* and in ancient Indian **anti** – *the opposite; before; earlier.*)

It was always used in European languages in the form of a preposition of negation-contraposition. However, it was never encountered in the postposition.

Its origin is unknown. (*1001 Words will present the sign of this word and its passport.*)

This formant-word played a particular role in Slavonic grammar. It came after other verb endings and, in negating the name, it derived the last form of the verb - the infinitive: - **anti > ati.**

The dropping of the nasal sound in this situation is a standard pattern in Slavonic phonetics. Prior to this, however, the formant would have been used to create antonyms that you cannot see without graphical signs. The Dictionary will relate in greater detail about the [proto-hieroglyph] ⌒ ***krov** – *shelter, roof, refuge* and its opposite: ⌣ ***krov-anti > krovat'** – *bed, loge, lair.* And about other antonyms as well.

CARTWHEELS AND FLIPS OF THE OX

It is not by chance that I cite this example which, it would seem, is a long way from our African subject matter of *negation by overturning:* such a revolution of the sign can be seen in this instance as well. And it was derived by priests of a Slavic tribe. However, they used not the inflexion of negation but the alternation of the vowel quality - soft/hard.

< – lev

∧ – lov

So how could this sign have been used in a practical sense? For a long time, in the Steppes of southern Russian, hunters' embankments were preserved, built in angular form. They were called "Serpents' embankments". In the Middle Ages, herds of wild horned cattle were rounded up, forced into the corner and caught. This could have been one of the applications of the obtained sign. And the word thus obtained became the root for others: лови – *lovi,* meaning *catch,* ловец – *lovets*, meaning catcher, ловкий – *lovkiy,* meaning *nimble.*

The form **lov** in the *hunting* sense is present in all Slavonic languages. But it is not found in any other language. Only in the neighbouring Lithuanian do we find anything similar: **lavus** – *nimble, deft*, or **lavyti** – *to exercise, to develop*. We look for words at least with the initial consonant the same and with a meaning that is not the total opposite. We consider the gothic, ancient Icelandic **laun** – *award*, Latin **lucrum** – *winnings, prize*, Irish **luaq** – *praise*. Etymologists find themselves having to see all these finds as related to the Slavonic **lov.** (Fasmer II, p. 508).

...In another Slavic tribe, the labial consonant is pronounced more firmly and more vibrantly. They saw an outline of an elevation in the sign:

∧ lob

From development of the semantics of this lexeme we are left with – **лобное место** [**lobnoe mesto** – *place of execution*] i.e. an *elevated place* (Rus.) and **лоб** – [**lob** – *forehead*], *the highest part of the body* > *head* > *skull* (Ancient Rus. **льбъ** – [l'b'] *skull*, [Slovak] **lob** – *skull, forehead*.

On this occasion, it would appear that Fasmer found genuinely related words in Indoeuropean languages: Greek **lofos** – *crest of a hill, hill*, Tocharian **lap** – *skull, head*.

Bernecker (1, 748 and [...]) and Specht (87) speak against comparing with the Greek **lofos**. But compare **взлобок** – [vzlobok – *hurst*]. (F, II. 507).

In the Greek lofos and the Russian **взлобок** we can see the outline of a graphical sign; this now gives words a greater evidence of kinship.

YET ANOTHER AFRICAN

The sign of an elevation with a name tends to "wander" in pre-Slavonic cultures. In some dialect, the end consonant is pronounced m¬¬ore aphonically:

< – lop

We will not waste time searching for words that are derived from this lexeme in other environments. What is more important now is to look at the effect caused by turning a sign that has been adopted into a non-Slavic culture:

v – * anti- lop

Only in Central Africa are there animals with such moon-shaped horns - antelopes (Latin **antilopa, antilopus**).

WE WANDER TO MEET OURSELVES, RECOGNISING OURSELVES IN OTHERS

Humans very early on found a way to name all the representatives of the Animal Kingdom. They named themselves, in fact, and humans merely listened closely to them (by symbolising sounds). Now we can see how they could been called by another method (by symbolising signs). These artificial names are just as resilient as their natural names. Humans named their brothers in nature a long time ago. And yet they named themselves last.

For all the resilience of the lexical forms, we can see that in the given examples, the most susceptible to phonetic changes proved to be the consonants.

Labial consonants have shown the full chain of development in the dialects: **f – w – v – b – p.**

Most likely, the flowing *l* was also subjected to changes. Therefore, when we speak of the eternal nature of the word, we allow for the entire range of phonetic evolutions of sound. Phonetically speaking, *l* may develop only to the extent of another flowing example (we have already seen the transformation of alfa > arfa).

Let us imagine the possibility of such transformations of sound in our particular instance:

∧ lob > rob

Ancient Russian **робъ** – **[rob'** – *slave, servant*]; **роба** – [**roba** – *slave girl*]. (The word is not presented in Western Slavonic and Southern Slavonic.) Derivatives: робеть [robet' – *to be shy*]; робить [robit'] – *to work*, in the Archangelsk, Vologda, Olonets, Vyatsk, Perm, [тяз. *Ryazan*????], Kaluga and Smolensk dialects (Dal').

Native Russian. In old Slavonic **рабъ - [rab']**. The form was likewise not spread into other Slavonic languages. The outline of the sign coincided with the pose of *grief* and the *fading of the moon*. Prostration, when a person touches the ground with the tips of their fingers, halves the human figure. It humbles and belittles the person. This characteristic was used earlier in religious rituals and in the social differentiation of society.

And it had to be reflected in the graphic signs, too. The fact that specifically this meaning (раб – rab) was already in the content of the name of the sign ∧ *rob (*rop), tells us of its direct antonym: ∨ *anti-rob (rop) > *antrop – *not a slave; a free man*. It remained in the Greek vocabulary: **antropos** – *man*. Exultant hands cast up represent the anti-sign of prostration. Early man first named all the animals, then the dependent slave and finally himself, the free man.

THE SLAVE [*RAB*] AND THE MAIN ARAB

In Ancient Western Asia, the Slavs conversed with the ancestors of the Arabs. The Arabs, in their own way, broke down the compound sign of the Ox. They did not see a negation in the later Line of the sign: in the Semitic languages the word was not controlled by inflexions and so the grammar of negation was not so expressed in the Semitic word as it was, say, in Ancient European or Turkic languages.

The pre-Arabic priest saw a symbol of society in 'alef – a combination of the signs of Master and Servant. However, when analysing the composition of the sign, he did not know how to split this name into two. Therefore, in the main component, as he saw it (the vertical line), he conveyed the overall name:

◄ – 'alef

Ӏ – **'alef** – *khalif* [caliph] (*khalef).

The second detail, opposite in meaning was named using the word flipped over: ◄ – **fela'** > **felakh**. In Arabic countries today this is what a working peasant is called. Initially, though, if not a slave, then the person was called a *rabotyaga*, a servant or the common people. And their sign of reverence was evidently accepted as prostration, only not right down to the ground.

In the etymological passport, when specifying the dates of birth of these words, we should also allow for the following circumstance. All palindromes probably arose mechanically in the early times of mastering the alphabetic script, when the direction of the line often changed. And the alphabetic signatures beneath pictures or on the plinths of sculptured images made more recently, could have been read in reverse. Such overturned words should be called **mechanical palindromes**. In the case at hand, the flipping of the word was made clearly with intention (**an artificial palindrome**), which was probably possible to make orally in the event of the flipping of a short word. However, here we can see that a polyphonic structure had to be mirrored. And to do this orally would hardly have been possible with such accuracy by placing the sounds in the reverse order. Most likely such work was done in the period of the alphabet, but before the advent of Arabic script (meaning before the 7th century of the Common Era). The data can be clarified by tracing the advent and the spread of the words *caliph* and *felakh* in the vocabularies and written monuments of other Semitic peoples.

To a certain extent it is helpful to compare the Arabic method of analysing this sign with the experience in creation of such a coupling of Master and Servant in Slavic culture However, instead of a palindrome, the Slavs used the now familiar method of alternating the soft and hard vowels.

◄ – 'alef > *khalep,

I – *khalep > khlib, khlip.

The first (social meaning) of the Line was not preserved. The naturalistic, sign-based meaning came out on top: **хлибый [khlibiy]** – *feeble, weak,* Archan. **хлибкий [khlibkiy]** – ditto (Eastern Russian) Fasmer: *unclear* (F. IV, 244).

The meaning of the derivative survived:

< *халоп, хлоп [khalop, khlop]

Ancient Russian **холопъ [kholop']** – *groveller, slave, serf* (the same in Ukrainian and Bulgarian). From Eastern Slavonic the word spread into other Slavonic languages. Fasmer: "All existing etymologies are unreliable... We have to reject the comparison with Ancient Indian jalpati – *speaks unclearly, mutters,* jalmas – *reprobate, scoundrel, base* (Maced.), also came closer to the literary silpti – *to become weak* ([Mazenauer]), from the German Schalk – *rogue, jester* ([Bruchner] *kinship* with пахолок and холить [to care for] is *incorrect* (F. IV. 257)

THE CODE OF THE WORD

THE PHILOSOPHY OF THE BEGINNING.
THE FIRST OPPOSITION

We can now imagine where the culture that was expressed in scripture and the word began life.

Africa. Moon worship. The [Priest] reduces the extreme phases of the Moon to an expression of the human age.

∪ – *the nascent moon – the beginning of life*
∩ – *the fading moon – the end of life*

It is with this ingenious graphical opposition that the spiritual culture began life; the recognition of the "twoness" of the world, consisting of an eternal system of contrasting points. Pictures of natural contraposition were transformed into a written grammar of negation through symbols of weapons:

∩ = Ψ ϴ ∪

Fading Moon = Slain Moon

The identity of forms of negation lies at the heart of cultural diversity. And it is in terms of these signs that we can judge how long ago independent cultural solutions appeared even in closely related ethnoses. The written language of one tribe preferred to apply the traditional image of the departing moon while, in the neighbouring tribe, its departure was decisively accelerated by the *spear,* the *arrow* or the *stone.* The etymologist has to consider the possibility of this variation when encountering homonyms such as the Russian **ropa [gora]** – *an elevated place* ∩ and the Bulgarian **ropa [gora]** – *forest* Ψ. Symbols of the first opposition were supplemented further as recognition of the world around developed.

∪ – young moon – moon – light – youth, life.
∩ – fading moon – darkness – death = Ψ ∪ – slain moon – not the moon – sun.

lucky horseshoe that should be nailed to the door, the entrance to a house, the residents of which wish each other a long and happy life. Nailed in place, but facing up and not the other way around, as we often observe in different parts.

The sign of death was embodied in a burial mound, in an urn bearing ashes and in a grave with an aspen stake.

Based on the signs of the First Opposition, pairs of meanings were distributed: light – dark, day – night, up – down, warm – cold, sky – earth…

And not always did the sign of the young moon designate the highest object.

For example,

⌣ *bůh – *bog* [god] (**byk* [bull])

⌢ *ne-bůh – *не бог [*ne bog – not god*] > небо [*nebo - sky*] (the opening of the last syllable, like in спаси бог [*spasi bog - save us, Lord*] > спасибо - [*spasibo - thank you*]).

These signs accompanied humans, filling their lives with new forms and new content.

⌣ ⌢ – *comedy and tragedy*. The symbol of the theatre.

It is more difficult to decipher the symbol of the human age in the conjunction

 ෆ ✧ ⊐ ✗ ⇄ ʕ etc.

In China this opposition gave rise to the philosophy of yin and yang.

The priests embodied the interpretation in the meaning of *man-woman* in rituals of joining the sexes – an *embrace*, *a kiss* and the *coital position*. They were supposed to take place at night, under moonlight, so that the divinity could see the attempts of the disciples to perform the testaments of the lunar constitution.

And every night in February
A candle burned upon the table,
A candle burned.

Pasternak. [not Mandelstam - *Мело весь месяц в феврале, И то и дело Свеча горела на столе, Свеча горела.*] February Revolution in Russia. The poet, in place of suffering on the squares, chose to use the image of the moon. In Ancient Greece lovers would make love until the oil in the lamp had run dry. *While the candle is burning* (from the song).

With another meaning (*Horns, Bull*), the lunar sign gained the opposite interpretations only episodically.

⌣ *bull*
⌢ *non-bull – pollard – hump-backed.*
ψ ʊ ʋ (and the sharply angular variations) *non-Bull – Cow – Calf – Ox*. Thus, the established identity of signs and meanings *Slain Moon – Sun = Slain Bull – Cow, Calf, Ram, Ox, Camel* helps us get to the bottom of the semantic code of the word.

Perhaps the ⚹ **'alef** in some primitive culture was also a hieroglyph of the Sun and, become widespread, it influenced the spiritual cultures.

However, one lexeme could not be held at once in the two first meanings in any one dialect *(bull = moon, cow = sun)*. Language rids itself of such homonyms in the very first instance. Leaving the lexeme with only one meaning. Now, though, we can allude in the names of the *Sun creatures* to the former meaning – *Sun*, in the names of the bull – the former names of the moon. Such an understanding can recover the graphic sign of the word. (For example, the Turkic uj, ud, ut – cow, identical to the Sumerian ➤ **ud** – *sun*. This means that at one time there was ➤ **ud** – 1) *cow*, 2) *sun* (Turkic, Sumerian).

THE EPIC OF THE MOUNTAIN OF GRIEF
[GORA GORYA]

In certain languages words must have been retained that were previously the names of the signs of the First Opposition. And probably in more than one language.

I have found such examples in Turkic-Oghuz dialects and I reunite them with graphemes:

∪ **ol** – *be, live* (Turkic, Azerbaijani, Turkmen.)

∩ **öl'** – *die* (Turkic, Azerbaijani, Turkmen.)

In Turkic-Kipchak, this opposition differed from the Oghuz:

∪ **bol** – *be, live* (Kazakh and others),

Ψ **böl'** – 1) *die, 2) *share, divide* (Kazakh and others).

(The initial labial in the languages, with a powerful inertia of the closed syllable had become weaker and was reduced. The Oghuz languages love the closed syllable, while the Kipchak languages love the open version) The first meaning of the Kipchak **böl'** was the mirror opposite of the initial **bol**. The Slavs at that time, it appears, adopted the sign of the slaying of the Bull-Moon and the name that became the word with the meaning expressing the concept, close to that of the original – *death of the divine animal* – **боль [bol']** – *pain*. Fasmer: "Similar to Old High German balo – *destruction, evil*, Old English bealu – *wickedness.*" F. I, 191. (Turkic materials are nearer and more conclusive: they are supported with signs).

Changing latitudes. *The African Moon* is not recognised and the priests of the new generation reconsidered the signs. And the consonant was developed: l > r:

∪ **or** – *moat, pit* (Kazakh and others)

∩ **ör** – *elevated place* (Kazakh and others)

In the Slavonic language the prosthetic consonant **h** opens the syllable. And the lexical meaning of the external flexion is rejected.

⌣ hor

⌢ hor-a[7]

In enunciatory practice the negating formant, too, acquires the prosthetic consonant that opens the syllable: wa > ba > pa... Such negating suffixes have been preserved in many languages.

The external inflexional word in dialects officially developed more actively than the internal inflexional word. This is evident in the example in question.

⌢ hor-a > hor-wa > hor-ba > hor-pa...

There are plenty of derivatives from these word models in Slavonic languages. In Russian lexemes are gathered both with a vibrant beginning and with an aphonic beginning:

```
              gor-a > gorb(a) > grob(a) > grb...
hor-a         khor-a > khor-wa...
              kor-a > korwa > krow(a)...
```

But why have the terms gorb, grob, krow and grib lost their vowel ending? Obviously not for reasons associated with grammar. This could have occurred only in one instance: if a tribe had joined the ranks of the Slavs, in whose language a powerful inertia of the closed syllable was manifested. And words that were deprived of their vowel ending form the essence of the legacy of the time when for a while the enunciatory tradition of the newcomers prevailed. This could have been a Germanic tribe.

---

[7] The Slavs in another dialect also used a different formant – j, which gives rise to the word **rope [grief]**, which speaks of the first meaning of the anti-sign.

THE ITALIAN REFLEX:

When assimilating an adopted word, the juncture of consonants that closes off a syllable is transformed into a long (doubled) consonant that opens a syllable.

This pattern has been present in Italian to this day. Latin words that have recently entered Italian: doctor > dottore, advocat > avvocato... and so on.

The second consonant in the juncture is doubled; the consonant that should open the syllable. Of all the European languages only Italian has such a powerful inertia of the open syllable, probably dating back to the very beginning of the age of writing.

*mům-ha (ᴪ) – **mucca** – *cow* (Italian), probably the oldest name for this animal.[9]

The Indoeuropeans should have long since discovered this pattern for themselves. The *Italian Reflex* is the most explicit expression of the rebuilding of the syllable. A process that has been developing with varying degrees of intensity in all dialects of the world. It is time that linguistics began to agree that the first classificatory indicator of any language should be acknowledged as the primary structure of the syllable. This is because, otherwise, we cannot understand the reasons for many phonetic patterns in the languages of the world. Even the advent of one pattern, the Italian reflex, has enabled us to see clearly what was taking place in the dark corners not only of the history of the word, but of the history of humankind as whole.

For example: HCC asserts that Latin arose earlier than all the Romance languages. Italian arose sometime in the Middle Ages from so-called Vulgar Latin. We will attempt to assert that all words with double vowels entered Latin from pre-Italian dialects, because Latin happily acknowledges even the most improbable junctures of consonants, loves the closed syllable more than the open syllable and, therefore, could not derive double consonants. And such words as terra – *land,* vacca – *cow* and gibba – *hump* arose not in the Middle Ages, rather they are encountered in the very earliest monuments. This means that Italian could then influence the Latin vocabulary. Sign-based etymology indicates that this took place even before the advent of the alphabetic script.

There is a certain confusion that can be observed in etymological dictionaries of the Italian language: how, for instance, can we explain the transformation of the Latin *gibba* into the Italian *gobba – hump*? But science makes provision for no other variation for the advent of the Italian word. Only *from Vulgar Latin!* And it is well known how it occurred in Latin – *the sign is arbitrary.* But no, it is not arbitrary.

This is what we suggest:

⌒ ***gorba > gobba** – *hump* (Italian)

In another pre-Italian dialect this same effect occurred when the vernacular Slavonic form was adopted: ***girba > gibba.** And this formation is what entered the Latin. The example confirms that the Slavonic **gorb** at one time had a vowel ending.

EASTERN ROMANCE LANGUAGE

Rome, before it conquered Europe, travelled East, reaching the warm climes of India. It brought its polytheism with faith in the supreme godhead *Devus-Piter (the *younger brother* of Jupiter). In Ancient Indian (Sanskrit) this name in the form of Diavus-pitar preserved even the Latin masculine ending – us, something the Indoeuropeans failed to notice. (In Ancient Indian the masculine ending is -a and the feminine is -ā, or -i.)

---

[9] I have offered a sign for the cow here, looking back at the Ancient Chinese hieroglyph: ¥·- *cow* (second millennium before the Common Era) Name unknown.

Put simply, the name of the god was brought from Rome. And the missionaries of this religion were Italians: in the Sanskrit dictionary many Latinisms are presented in Italian pronunciation. Why not verify this version? One of the most important Latin terms that entered the Ancient Indian language had first-hand experience of the impact of the Italian reflex.

What is Sanskrit? It is the language of those who brought the faith in the god Diavus-pitar. This is what all Ancient Indian authors tell us. It is the language of religion and the language of sacred books. And what is *Sacred writing* in Latin? **Sanct-scriptum.** And how do Italians pronounce this term? They write it just as they pronounce it: **San-scritto.**

The Brahmin missionaries were unable to overcome all the junctures of the consonants, but they significantly simplified the pronunciation, by opening the last two syllables. I think this is how the word occurred, for which so many etymologists seek conformity in the Indian languages. In the course of a little over two millennia it, of course, has given rise to some new words in that environment, but the derivatives are too closely tied in to superficial meanings of the term and cannot even hint at its first meaning. Yet its first meaning, it transpires, lies in Latin-Italian: **sanscritto > sanscrit.** As we now know, the loss of the end vowel occurs in a language that is drawn to the closed syllable.

THE SYLLABIC PALINDROME

The epic tale of the sign *Gora* continued into the age of syllabic writing. The clay tablet (we assume) depicted the sign *Gora* and below it wrote out the name in syllabic graphic elements. (This is how the ancient Semitic dictionaries, the syllabaries, appeared, thanks to which we can see the Sumerian hieroglyphs and learn their names. The practice of such vocabularies must have been widespread in the multi-ethnic Ancient World.)

⌒ **gor-ba.** Let us assume it is written from left to right.

Those whose read and wrote from right to left would have read the signs in reverse order: **ba-gor**. Perhaps this is how the mechanical syllabic palindrome arose – **bagor** – with is main meaning of *hook*. Subsequently, too, as a result of the Slavonic labialisation (when the root vowel assimilates the prepositional vowel) it is derived in a dialect – **bugor** – *hill* (Russian).

The mechanical syllabic palindrome is a new phenomenon, to which the attention of etymologists must be focused. Words like this, if they are not alone in a dictionary, prove that the language cognised the period of syllabic writing.

For example, in the Chuvash language there is the word **vak**ar – *cow*, which may be compared with the possible Slavonic archetype: **va-car = car-va** – *cow*. I would have passed this parallel by if it had not been for another signal: **porto** – *topor [axe]* (Chuvash) And here the parallel certainly suggests itself: **por-to = to-por**. It resembles a system. This means the parallels intersect. And for now it is not important if the authors of these words were Turkic-Chuvash or Slavs. What is important is that both these ethnoses made use of syllabic writing. *1001 words* will demonstrate artificial syllabic palindromes, when syllables, when read in reverse, offer another meaning for a word. The opposite of the original meaning. In other words, the artificial syllabic palindrome, as with the letter form, was a grammatical means for creating antonyms.

BEFORE ADAM AND EVE

Priests gave names first to the lunar animals and then to those devoted to the sun, with humans coming last. In naming humans they used the very same set of signs and their names. A number of the "humanised" hieroglyphs found their way by chance into the Phoenician alphabet. Looking at their forms, we can understand the train of thought of the authors of the symbols, de-termine the grammatical resources they used and the rules governing symbol creation.

Here I highlight a pair of related letters:

∃ - he

⊟ - ḥet

In the pre-Greek alphabet they are presented in the form:

Ǝ - e

𐌁 - ē

The additional line on the left is perceived as a diacritical sign of the increase (of the length) of the sound. In the [eastern] (Avestan) alphabet, the length of the vowel was also ex-pressed by a vertical line, joined with the main sign, only directed downwards:

➤ u ➤ ū

In Late Greek and Latin, the length was expressed by a horizontal line, not connected to the main letter: ā, ū ...

In this way, two means of designating the length of the sound are determined. We will call them provisionally the *Eastern* (unified) and the *Western* (analytical). Here, the line has no name, only a function. In the sign that entered the Phoenician alphabet the vertical line had both a function and a name, which is easily determined: - *t.

This pair entered the Phoenician alphabet from some hieroglyphic script that is now un-known. However, if these are former hieroglyphs, then their names, without doubt, came to be words of one of the languages of the Ancient World. Most likely regions of Ancient Western Asia or Asia Minor. But not Egypt and not Sumer, because no such pair is found in their hiero-glyphs. Archaeologists have yet to uncover all the treasures of antiquity in these regions. The 19th century, the century of archaeology, revealed the civilisations of Sumer, Akkadia and Babylon, the Hittites and the Luwians.

However, considerably more cultures were dissolved in the clay soils of these territories. And we encounter fragments of one of them in the Phoenician alphabet. Their names and the forms of the symbols help to reveal the necessary words in existing dictionaries. I will not de-scribe the search process in all its finer details, but I will give an overview.

First, it appears, the following pair was created:

ꓷ(**>**) - *ůŋ - *hůŋ – 1) *Moon*; 2) *Bull* > *Husband, Master, Head of the Family*

ꓱ(**ꓱ >**) - *eŋ > heŋ – 1) *Non Moon - Sun*; 2) *Non Bull (Cow, Calf. Ox, Ram)* > *Non Husband (Family, Wife, Serf* (commoner)*, Human)*.

The names of the compound sign clearly differed in their morphology: some were formed by external inflexion, others by internal inflexion. The naming of the Phoenician letters **he** and **het** were classed under the variant with internal flexion.

CHINESE HUMAN

At this stage this pair of symbols could have entered the scripture of the pre-Chinese, who we believe lived in the regions of Mesopotamia in the third millennium before the Common Era.

One of the pair of hieroglyphs appeared in Ancient Chinese scripture, monuments of which can be found on the shores of the Pacific Ocean: ➤ - *human* (name unknown), second millennium before the Common Era. Several centuries later the hieroglyph appears in Chinese writing in the following form: 人 人 - **žen'** – *human*.

Sinologists hesitate in admitting that this sign was called the same in Ancient Chinese because of their conviction, generally accepted in linguistics, that no word can live for more than two thousand years. And yet the word **žen'**- *human* has existed in Chinese for more than two millennia, so no one has resolved to increase its age by another two.

And we will see where it arose: in the Far East, or was it brought there from Ancient Western Asia? The results of this search should help to recover the name of this Ancient Chinese hieroglyph.

The priests in pre-Latin cultures also worked with the sign ➤ - **gen**, but already without its first meanings. That is why they interpreted it through association with images of items. For example, they saw in it a *leg bent at the knee*. The internal dash as if marked a certain part of the leg and it was to this part that the name **gen** was given. Can we not, therefore, see the word **genu** – *knee* (Latin) as appearing in the same way?

In another tribe, the priest saw that the internal dash pointed as if to the upper part of the cheekbone: **gena** – *the upper part of the cheek near the jugal bone* (Latin).

In an Albanian tribe, however, the priest actually saw a gaping mouth with a fang: **gen** – *dog* (Albanian). And so on and so forth.

The Birth of Bowing

Now I will determine to recover the etymological history of the Ancient Chinese hieroglyph.

>   gen
> – *hen   khen
>   ken

Ancient Western Asia

Third Millennium BCE

➤ - *gen >*žen' - *human* (commoner)   Ancient China,

                                                        Second millennium BCE

人 𠆢 - žen- *human*   China
                                                      First millennium BCE - present day

Such was the force of the graphic sign that, when encountering another, the Ancient Chinese tried to write, depict the sign **žen** with their bodies – bending at the waist, holding their joined elbows to their chest. Showing that he is a *žen*, meaning a *human, one of us*, in other words. That he is not a master to the man he encounters, but a humble servant. All commoners would bow to their masters and to one another, thus acknowledging mutual respect and loyalty. And the masters would also bow to one another, only holding their hands down by their sides.

This is how scripture formed a steady ritual of žen - a characteristic symbol of Chinese culture that spread widely across Southeast Asia together with the scripture.

Although the bow, as a sign of submission and reverence, occurred in the western part of the most ancient Eurasia. We have seen how the symbols ◂ **felah** and ◂ **holop** occurred.

However, they differed from the Chinese, primarily in their position. This is what an old (fading) moon looks like.

The Chinese, though ▸ (Э-) – is a young, northern moon, transformed by the *spear-arrow of negation* into an old, *slain* version. The gesture known as namaste, with the hands placed together in front of the chest, occurred in an attempt to depict the internal detail of the sign *žen.*

THE TURKIC READING OF
THE CHINESE SYMBOL FOR *HUMAN*

...The Turkic people saw this hieroglyph but they understood it too forthrightly: **žen'** – [*be victorious*] (Kazakh). They also encountered the variation: ▸ - **žen**[10] even with a *shiny dot*, which they had the fortune to see on the shores of some warm seas, when pearls were extracted. And they named this shiny dot descriptively: ***žen-išik** – inside (the sign) *žen*.

The Turkic people (Kipchaks) pronouncing the **že** sound passed the name of the pearl to those who pronounced only the **e** sound. In Orkhon-Yenisei texts we encounter **jänčü** – жемчуг [*zhemchug - pearl*]; Azer. indži; Chuvash. endže. But the Ancient Russian женчуг [*zhenchug*] and Ukrainian женчуг [*zhenchug*], жемчуг [*zhemchug*] proved nearer to the initial form.

In Ancient Russian it is encountered starting from the 12th century. Fasmer: *Probably of Chinese origin* (F.II, 46). The root of the word is indeed similar to the Chinese word. The second part, though, was added by the Turkic people. There were sufficient words accepted by the Eastern Slavs with this formant for the diminutive suffix – **ičik, -išik** to appear in their language – (*mal-ičik – мальчик [*boy*], *stul- ičik – стульчик [*small stool*], укол – укольчик [*small jab, prick*] and so on)

All of these examples contradict the generally accepted HCC, but our task for now is simply to state the facts. To find them and state them.

HOW ELSE CAN WE EXPRESS RESPECT AND VENERATION?

In summary, we return once more to the opposition of *Муж – мужик, Господин – раб [Master and Servant]*...- the very first sign-based alternatives and identities:

In sign terms: >< = >≽ (>▶)
⊃⊂ = ⊃D (Э Ǝ)

The compound sign with the *spear*, now without the *opposing simple sign* became especially widespread. It is interpreted as a syncretical form of opposition - *the people is a unity of opposites.* We can see such an understanding in the Proto-Arabic *overturned* sign ◀ **'alef**. Standing out from it are ❘ - **caliph** (master) and ◀ **filah** (servant).

The pre-Savs adopted the sign with the name and analysis from their then neighbours in Ancient Western Asia: ❘ - *халип [khalip] > хлип [khlip]* (master). And ◀ *холоп [khol-op], хлоп [khlop]* (serf, servant).

Evidence of the close acquaintance of the Slavs with the Semitic pronunciation of the word *'alef ('alip)* is evidenced in the preserved initial, weak, guttural consonant which the Greeks, for example, did not pronounce and thus obtained the word *alpha*.

... I believe that the pre-Italians knew the variation of ➤ -*gen* – *human*. In this meaning the word existed in European dialects and its traces are preserved in compound terms in English: **citizen** (from the word **city**), in French: *gendarme* (in transcription - žan d'arm – *an armed man*) and others.

---

[10] The outline *(spear, arrow)* in other scriptures alternated with the Point of Negation *(stone, wound)*

The Italians, though, saw another meaning in the sign - lowering oneself in a bow is a manifestation of respect and not simply subservience.

In the West at that time, the sign of increase (the multiplier) was applied. For this use was made (judging by the name) of the Sumerian hieroglyph ↑ **ti (tir, til)** – *arrow*. * ❯ ↑ - *****gen – til** – *high respect.*

This is probably how the word **gentile** – *polite*, **gentilmente** – *politeness* (Italian), possibly brought by the Roman cohorts into the British Isles, where *popular etymology* transformed the word into **gentleman**.

THE SUMERIAN ARROW IS STILL IN FLIGHT
(ABOUT THE GREAT AND THE ABJECT)

At the end of its flight it entered the alphabets.

↑ - ti (Coptic script of the 3rd Century CE)

↑ - t (Gothic 4th Century CE)

Naturally related to the Latin T t and the Greek T

However, despite this, we cannot fail to allow also for the Late ↑ Sumerian hieroglyph - **ti (til, tir)**, which in other hieroglyphic systems (which have not survived to this day) could have been applied in simplified form - without the feathers ( ) and even without the arrowhead (**I**), but nonetheless preserving t ↑ Sumerian name. And somewhere the very first pre-Sumerian ***j** > **i** itself was also preserved. Such an *arrow without feathers* reached the Phoenician alphabet **I** - **j** (jota) (2nd millennium BCE) and Chinese script as well: the horizontal **i** – *one, unit*.

... The Slavs also had to use such a form of sign-based opposition: **I —** . The vertical designated an active social personality; the horizontal, a passive one. Based on the meanings of the words we could recover both the symbols and their names, which became determinative words.

I - *tel

— - *nik

Учи-тель [Uchi-tel - *teacher*] – a socially active figure.
Учи-ник > **ученик** [Uchenik - *student*] – a socially passive figure.

Terms that come with the determinative -*tel earlier expressed genuinely elevated meanings, designating the elite in society - *sviatitel* [*sanctifier*], *skazitel* [*fabulist/narrator*], *voitel* [*warrior*], *povelitel* [*sovereign*]... In any event, the Slavs still remembered the hieroglyphic script. Later the positive meaning of the formant was lost, although such heroes cannot be classed as passive examples: *ochernitel* [*vilifier*], *pokhititel* [*kidnapper*], *muchitel* [*tormentor*]...

*tel did not become an independent word in the Slavonic languages (such, for example, as **tel** – *elevated place* in Ancient Yiddish), but the sound combination **nik** was more fortunate. It appeared in the formants and it also became a word in its own right: with a meaning the opposite of the meaning of the vertical. Russian gathered dialectic forms – *ник [nik]*, *нич [nich]*, *низ [niz]*, *ниц [nits]*. Etymological dictionaries of the Russian language consider each of these words separately: they see them as being unrelated. And an individual history is offered for each of them. (Fasmer, III, 73-75.) Now, though, when the Vertical **(tel)** – Horizontal **(nik)** opposition is restored, grounds arise for genuine etymology.

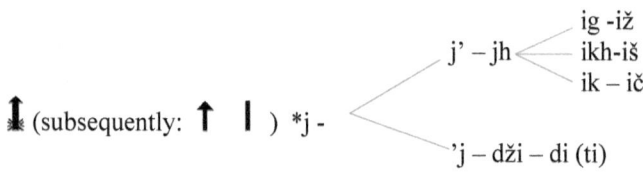

In certain dialects of Mesopotamia in the 3rd to 2nd millennia, the names of the *arrow* acquired forms that were less and less similar to one another. The line could be read both as i and as d and t. Or as a more developed ti, with a closed syllable tin and then (NLR) – til – tir. Which is what happened in Sumerian itself.

For the pre-Slavs in one of the dialects, where there was ⏐ ik (ič) *overturning* the arrow, using the negation ni, the opposite is created: ━ ***ni - ik>nik (nič)**. In a neighbouring dialect: Vertical – **ig (iž, iz)**, Horizontal – **ni – iž(niž, niz)**. Ник [nik], низ [niz], нич [nich], ниц [nits] - all of these words meant one and the same thing in the Slavonic dialects - *non-height*. If the first (in this instance) name of the vertical had been preserved, it would have had a very specific concept: ***ik** – *high, elevated, up*. Such pairs of *unmasked antonyms*, however, do not remain in a language for long. And one of the parts is replaced, which makes the opposition stronger.

This is how the system was formed: **|** - **tel, ▬- nik**, actively used in Slavonic languages. Still unnoticed by Slavists.

Now, though, when the signs and the genesis of these names are recovered, the opportunity arises to etymologise what would appear at first glance to be the most hopeless lexemes, which have no correspondences in neighbouring or more remote languages. And Old Russian also falls into this category - **нищь [nishch']** – *poverty-stricken* (an extremely expressive application of the symbol of a socially passive personality), and **нить [nit']**. Etymological dictionaries cite examples that, again, only serve to demonstrate the hopelessness of the method of phonetic correspondences: old Indian **nivis** *loincloth,* [Old High German] **najan** – *to sew,* Latin **neo** – *to spin, to weave,* old Indian **snauati** – *to swathe, to dress* and so on (Fasmer, III, 76). All of these meanings are related in some way to the semantics of the word *nit'* [*thread*] and the words almost all begin with the nasal consonant. However, it should not be considered that this is insufficient for the etymology of the word **nit'**. And of all others, too. Only the method of the **sign-based etymology** enables us to learn the true history of the word.

...The ancient creators of the word likewise did not forget the first meaning of the line – arrow. Thus there are meanings that confuse etymologists. Fasmer: "Derivatives from *****никнуть [*niknut']** are not always easy to distinguish" (F. III, 75).

He had in mind **никнуть [niknut']** – to wilt and **никнуть [niknut']** – *to pass or enter something or somewhere (to consider carefully, to penetrate).*

And in another dialect, from where the horizontal *arrow* had shot out, **nig > niž > niz**, it also gave rise to dual semantics: **низ [niz]** and **низать [nizat']** (пронизать [pronizat'] – *to pierce*, пронзать [pronzat'] – *to stab*, нанизать [nanizat'] to *thread* – , вонзить [vonzit'] – *to thrust*) and, eventually, came the noun **ниж [nizh]** – *knife* (Ukr.).

The Vertical and the Horizontal are presented more in languages than even the Vertical and the Angle. These symbols will *work* in many scriptures, both in a pair and on their own, obtaining different meanings and fulfilling different grammatical functions.

ADAM AND EVE?

To generalise, we can say that the very first oppositions of related symbols ⌣∩)((graphical variations ∧ ˅><) over the course of cultural development transformed into synonymous systems ⌣Ψ,)Ӡ (Ɒ ▶ ➤), which disintegrated in the age of the Sun worshippers: <u>the sign of the Moon could no longer come in a pair with the sign of the Sun</u>.

And so the sign of the Slain Moon (Sun) began its own life - Ψ Ӡ Ɒ ▶ ➤ Ǝ, which itself can be read as a mini-system of opposites – Line and Angle. A restructuring of the sign takes place, allocating opposite meanings to each part. In the end, each of these parts itself becomes the basis for a new system of opposites. Which we can see is what happened with the Line (*Spear, Arrow), which was transformed into the Vertical and the Horizontal – Up and Down.

However, it is probable that all variations of oppositional systems reached historical times in different cultures. Both the very first ⌣ ∩ (southern) and the northern) (with their principal meanings: Bull (husband) – Cow (wife). Most likely they retained the first metaphorical meaning that helped the priests see in them the first pair in humanity – Adam and his Eve, created from his **rib**. They were probably vested with many different names. Perhaps the Old Iranian **ad am** – *I am* is manifested in the biblical legend. We will get to Eve, although her symbol is known – *Adam's Rib*. The sign of Adam may be the same *rib*, only facing the opposite direction:). Or is it a Line? If it is a Line, then it is of course, a Vertical! Ɒ - one of the variations of the sign of the Sun. Then: I - Adam,) - Eva (*rib*, taken from Adam).

... The Egyptian legend on the origin of people. The forefather Atum (is this a variation in the pronunciation of the name Adam?) is spat out of the mouth of twins – a boy and a girl. It is from them that the human race originated. A sign coming from Sumerian script could have pointed the Egyptian priest onto such a subject: ⟩ - **ud** – *sun* (Sumerian). It could have been adopted without a name, so another was used. The oblique cross could well have expressed the concept of twins. The subject of the divine forefather twins was widespread in the legends of the Ancient World from where, in all likelihood, it was taken East. In his fundamental book, Grigorii Potanin, a researcher of the folklore of the Siberian people, often found this subject in genealogical legends (19th century). Gradually, the pair of different sexes became a pair of the same sex.

The Sumerian sign for the Sun was also interpreted as *the wolf's (dog's) mouth, bringing forth twins.* We recall the Capitaline She-Wolf, who suckled Romulus and Remus. As we see, they now have a different function – to found the great city of Rome. The Turkic people see their origin as either a wolf or the progenitor, the she-dog. In a number of Turkic peoples, until recently, a sick child would be placed near a suckling dog to be cured.

ON GENIUSES AND GIANTS

So, in the lunar age, a system of alternatives was created – *Bull – Cow:* ⌣ Ψ (Africa),) Ə (north) graphical variations ⟩ ⟩;] Ǝ. Metaphorical meanings: *Husband – Wife, Man – Servant (commoner) Forefather – Race.* But one of the first meanings: **Moon-Sun** *(Slain Moon)*

MAN WITH ARROW

In the age of the Sun, the sign of the Bull was excluded from the pair, because it also designated the Moon, and this was already a symbol of the paganism of that time. And a new pair arose, the basis of which was the compound sign of the Sun. Let us consider graphical variations that found their way into the Phoenician alphabet:

∃ - he
⊟ - het

Relying on information from dictionaries, we endeavour to recover the archetypes

∃ - hen
■ - henti (hen-j)

Approximate systems for the phonetic development of the root lexeme in dialects:

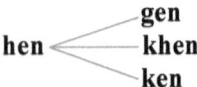

Based on these models, words appeared in the dialects of the Ancient World, in the regions of Mesopotamia and Asia Minor in the 3rd to the 2nd millennia before the Common Era, that speak of the high levels of cultures and the social development of the ethnoses.

In the Latin vocabulary there are terms that could have derived from the names of signs of the presented pair and so we will risk joining the words and graphemes, to understand the train of thought of the priest-interpreters, who assigned them meanings.

∃ - genus – *race* (***gen**) **human*
■ - gentis – *people, tribe* (***genti; gent**)

They did not forget that the hieroglyph **gen** at one time also meant *human* in the pre-Latin dialects. Evidence of this can be found in signs that allow us to assume the existence of a dialect in which the following words occurred:

∃ -- **gen** - * *human*
吕 -- **genti** > **gianti** – *large human, giant.*[11]

Middle English **giante** – ***giant***, German **Gigant** – ditto, Ital. **gigante** – *giant*. This word confirms that the meaning of the preceding **gen** was *human*. The Line (*arrow*) gave an increase in size, specifically to *him*.

In another dialect, the *arrow* was named not ***ti** , but using a more ancient name ***j**, although *human* was present there, too:

∃ - **gen** - * *human*
吕 - **gen -j** - *great human*[12]   Lat. **genius.**

It transpires that the ancestors of the Chinese recognised the written man with his back bent in a bow ➤**gen**, while the pre-Latin people recognised him with a straight back ∃ - **gen**. Naturally, this had an impact even on the ethnic (national) nature and on everything else that is connected with it in culture and psychology. The symbol expressed not only a disposition to bowing in reverence, but a flexibility, as one of the important conditions in the art of survival, in which the Chinese proved to be masters.

---

[11] Italian contains many examples of the Latin extension e>ia.
[12] Mention has already been made of the characteristic alternating of 'j -dži-di (ti) –d(t), that was manifested in many languages of the Ancient World.

AH, SAMARA – WHAT A TOWN

In a dialect with an unvoiced guttural, only the multiplication sign is worked on, from which, according to the law of twoness, an alternative is formed.

■ *kenti > kent -1) *tribe > 2)*small-town community> 3) *small town*.

The author of symbols removes the diminutive, forming a new anti-symbol and, accordingly, the name changes:

☐ *kanti > kant -1) *Large town, city*

This is derived in a dialect where the grammatical alternation of the quality of *hard/soft* sounds is adopted. The obtained words are used actively in Central Asia, where Iranian and Turkic peoples have long since lived side by side. Turkic names of small towns – Tashkent (*Stone Town*), Chimkent (*Town from the Soil*). Large cities: Sarkand (*Yellow City*), Kokand (*Sky-blue City*), Samarkand...

Samar is not a [Persian] and not a Turkic word. I believe its closest relative is **šaman**, which means *north*. The [Maia] took it from Ancient Western Asia, before it was transformed, [according to the law of NRL], into the Old Semitic **šamal** – *north*.

The Aramaeans, perhaps, perfected the process of developing the nasal ending into flowing: **šamar** – *north* (and also the old Semitic **ben** – *son*, in Aramaic **ber** which proves that one of the semitic languages had the preceding *bel – *son*).

And we can see how far north the Aramaeans reached by the spread of the word **samar** in the names of the towns and cities. Perhaps the Russian city of Samara is somehow related.

... How long ago did the terms **kent** and **kant** arise? The ancient Semites, who seized Mesopotamia in the 3rd millennium before the Common Era, made the Sumerian city of Akkad the capital of their new empire. Tractates call the ancient Semitic language Akkadian for the sake of convenience. However, not the Semitic, the Persian or any other languages of Mesopotamia help with the etymology of this word. We will make an assumption: ***Ak-kand** – *White City* (Turkic)

Of course, it would be more correct to voice such a version after the chapter Sumer-name, which presents lexical evidence of the Turkic and Sumerian cultural ties.

... The NRL law also appeared in works of the unvoiced dialect:

🔲 - **kent > kelt > kert**

The form of the word changed, but the meaning remained almost the same. The middle word **кельт [celt]**, which we know as an Ethnonym, has the lexical meaning of *tribe* or *people*. **Керт [kert]**, however, means *small town* (Arm.)

IN THE MIDDLE OR ON THE MARGINS – HETTITES AND HATTITES

Among peoples where the first sound in the name of a sign was pronounced with a *primary* guttural, the semantics of the grapheme barely differed from what came before.

◧ * **henti** - *our people, us*.

◻ **hanti** – *other people, *aliens, who surround us, or those who are the opposite of us*. Most often, the aliens proved to be the closest, almost kindred neighbours.

In those times, graphic formulae of ethnocentrism were born, ⊙ ◻ ◧ where every people saw themselves as surrounded by alien peoples. It is from here that the world was divided into the **мы** [us] and the **не мы** [not us]. Then came the *Cabbala,* then the *our nation in the centre of the world and the we are the hub of the universe.*

Today, China calls itself *Zhongguo* – the *Middle Kingdom*. And when written this name traditionally uses the hieroglyph ⊞ **džun**, meaning *middle*. The Turkic and Oghuz people described this symbol in the 7th century BCE when naming themselves, as reported in the Assyrian chronicles, **iškuz** (*isk-ūz, meaning *Inner Oghuz*). In the Oghuz epic *Dede Gorkut* the Oghuz actually called themselves **ičo-guz** (the *Inner People*), naming all others the **taš-oguz** the *Outer People*).

In the Turkic languages: **ūz, ouz, oguz** – the name the Turkic and Oghuz peoples gave themselves. An earlier meaning of the word is *people.*

And so firmly did this become embedded in the consciousness that ◻ **-hanti** was the Alien, the Opposite of Us, that the name of the symbol became a common word in its own right: **hanti** – *opposite* (Hittite), Lat. **anti**, Eng. **anti.**

... We will try the *Italian* Reflex. This is the name we provisionally give to the restructuring of the closed syllable into the open syllable, which occurs in a language with a powerful inertia of the open syllable when an adopted word with a different syllabic structure is assimilated. Of all the Indoeuropean languages the clearest trend is manifested in Italian. The junctures of the consonants that hamper the opening of the syllable are simplified or altogether transformed into a double consonant that opens the syllable. I return to the same examples as before, as to how the Italians rework Latin words in their enunciatory practice: doctor > dottore, advocat>avvocato, sanct-scriptum > san-scritto etc.

I am convinced that all Latin words with long (double) consonants came from ancient Italian dialects: **terra** – *earth*, **gibba** – *hump* and others. This is because in Latin there is no inertia of the primary syllable (be it open or closed), so syllables are not reworked in linguistic borrowings.

In Asia Minor, where it is considered that the family of Indoeuropean languages first arose and where even a relatively precise date is given – 2nd millennium BCE[13], there was an unknown dialect, similar to Italian, for which it was characteristic to restructure the syllable:

henti > hetti
hanti > hatti

Perhaps our structures will help to unravel the confusion that is hampering the determination of whether the Hittite scribes made mistakes in one and the same texts, when they referred to either the people known as the **hetti**, or to the people known as the **hatti**. Is it a misprint or was there really a people called the **hatti**?

---

[13] Tamaz Gamkrelidze, Vyacheslav Ivanov, *Indo-european language and Indoeuropeans, A Reconstruction and Historical Analysis of a Proto-Language and a Proto-*Culture vol. I and II. Tbilisi, 1984.

From the early 20th century, scholars have tried to understand these persistent *misprints.* Until they finally reached the decision that Hattite is really not an alien language, but proto-Hittite. Not everyone agrees with this. "The name proto-Hittite is widely used, but this could give rise to certain confusion, as it could appear that proto-Hittite is an early stage of Hittite when in fact these languages bear not the slightest relation to one another".[14]

I believe that ethnonyms such as **hanti, anti** and **hatti**, that we encounter in the history of scripture, are not names that peoples give themselves, but nicknames given by Central (Inner, Middle) ethnoses to neighbouring or simply alien, *marginal* tribes. The Roman historian Jordan, for instance, when speaking of battles of the Goths, names a tribe that was the opposite of the Goths, the Anti (in which Slavists saw the Slavs).

... ☐ **hanti** > **halti** > **harti** (NRL)

This symbol gained a multitude of figural meanings. The Latin **charta** – *paper* is directly related to it (earlier it is probable that this was a rectangular piece of writing material, such as parchment; Here the shape of the material and not the material itself was what was important). Then comes the Italian **carta** – *paper*, **cartina** – *a slip of paper*, **cartone** – *large paper.*

In a dialect with a voiced layngeal (g) the end dental (d) was also voiced, but the symbol, clearly, remained the same: Alb. garth – *fence, enclosure,* Lith. gardas – *enclosure.*

In the Slavonic languages there was a metathesis of the flowing element: Slovenian grad – *city, town* (initially – a large, enclosed settlement), Czech hrad, Serbo-Slav. град [grad].

---

[14] O.R. Gurney, *Hetti,* Moscow 1987. p. 111, translation into Russian (O.R. Gurney. The Hittites. Baltimore, Maryland, 1964).

A lesser settlement, we recall, was designated by a halving sign ⊟ and was named at the final stage of the phonetic development of the flowing elements **kert** (voiceless laryngeal) **gert', gerd'** (voiced). The latter, after the loss of the primary meaning, could have become the basis for the name of the central part of the sign (the middle of the body) in the Indoeuropean languages. At the same time the soft root was preserved better in a number of European terms: Herz – heart, сердце [serdtse] (Rus.), серце [sertse] (Bel. and other Slavonic languages), sirds (Latvian), širdis (Lith.). And in *the very oldest of the Indoeuropean languages* the root vowel had already hardened, like in the name of the *empty sign* **kard** – *heart* (Hittite).

The Slavs could see for themselves this sign and the line that divided it into two, which is why in one of the dialects the word **середина [seredina - *middle*]** (средина [sredina - *mean*]) came to be.

... The name of the Empty Sign also underwent phonetic reactions like the metathesis of flowing elements and delaryngation:

```
              anti – alti – lati
□ – hanti
              halti
```

Judging by the names, the biblical Chaldaea and the ancestors of the Latin peoples featured in the not us category. It could have crushed some while elevating and imbibing others with adrenaline. The lati people, fleeing in the 7th century BCE from the drought-ridden Asia Minor to the expanses of the Apennines, named this alternative environment by flipping their own name LATI to become ITAL, and then conquering it.

In this same age ethnonyms arose from these same mutually opposing heraldic symbols, which differ in the quality of the root vowels. In the names of closely related neighbouring countries of lietuva (Lithuania) and latvia (Latvia) this difference is clear to see. In the name of one nation, it would appear, the ungr and vengr, two closely related ethnic groups came together, at one time neighbouring, but mutually hostile.

THE MAN WITH AN ARROW IN SUMERIA

Now we can move a step closer to the Sumerian material.

ᛒ - **lu** – *human* (the *l* is soft and is palatalised).[15]

ᛒ ᛒ - **lulu** – *people, persons.*

This word gained popularity throughout the expanses of Ancient Western Asia, only with meanings that characterise the attitudes to the Sumerians on the part of their neighbours: **lulu** – *enemies* (Urartu), **lulu** – *alien people* (Old Persian). **Lulu** (liuliu) is the name given in Iran and Tajikistan to gypsies.

The first (Sumerian) meaning of the word could have been preserved only in the languages of ethnoses who were amicably disposed toward the Sumerians. These, it appears to transpire, were the Proto-Germanic people and the Early Slavs, in the dialectatic dialects of which the word, now transformed, has reached our time.

The Sumerians themselves created the plural through doubling. They were unable to apply their own hieroglyph for this purpose ↟ (↑) –ti **(til,tir).**

We will ascertain together in future which of the ethnoses that populated Ancient Western Asia was the first to succeed in doing this. For now we are gathering instances of the use of the *multiplication arrow.* A version: **ᛒ ↑**

- **lu-ti (lu-til, lu-tir) lu-j.**

We will take a look in the dictionaries. We find close correspondences only in the Germanic and Slavonic languages: **liut** – people (Old High German), **liute** (Middle German), **люди [liudi], люд [liud]** (Rus.). It is widespread in all Slavonic languages: **ludżie, lud** (Pol.), **l'udie, l'ud** (Old Czech), **lide, lid** (Czech), **ljudje, ljud** (Slovenian)

---

[15] The hieroglyph lu in Sumerian is decorated with six oblique lines that designate the numerical value of the hier-oglyph. They have no meaning here, though, and we present the symbol in simplified form.

Fasmer: "there are no grounds to speak of the Germanic origin of the word люд [liud], despite the writings of [Paiskerry], Trautman and Hirth" (Fasmer II , p. 545) .

However, there is also no mention of the Slavonic origin of the word. Only now are we finding any general sources.

[Note. If the Turkic people heard the lut words with a hard l, then they could have derived a metathesis of flowing elements *in Turkic* in their enunciatory practice. In other words, restructuring the open syllable into a closed one: **ult** – *people, nation* (in a number of Turkic languages, Kazakh and Karakalpak in particlar). In other Turkic languages there is the pleophony ulyt, ulut, olot, uluth, ulus-*tribe, people*]

The priests of a Slavic tribe saw the sign of the armed man and their reaction could have been expressed in the meaning the of the word **лютый [liutiy], лют [liut]** (Rus.), the Ukrainian лютий [liutiy], the Belarusian люты [liuty]– *angry, wicked*, the Bulgarian лют [liut], the Slovenian ljut, the Czech liti (arch. l'uty) and the Polish luty. No correspondences are found in other languages. There is likewise no etymology.

THE KNIGHT AND MUM

Germanic priests saw the sign of *Man with Weapon*, where the arrow appeared like a spear. In the tribe in the dialect of which they knew the name of the arrow **tir (ter)**, the written figure of the *armed ma*n was personified in the image of a warrior enfettered in armour. The hieroglyph pointed the pre-Germanic couturier to the form of armoured dress, which was initially made, we should assume, from tanned hides. (Such armour was still used in the Orient until relatively recently, protecting from both arrows and spears.)

People worthy of such protection were called in [Middle High German] rihter, in German ritter, in Old Czech ryter, in Czech ritir, in Polish rycerz, in Old Russian рыцерь [rytser'] and рицерь [ritser']. Nowadays: **рыцарь [rytsar'** - *knight*].

Etymology. **B ↑** - lu-tir > lu-ter > lyter (lyder)> ryter > ryhter> rytter…

The alternation of the vowels u/y is evident in the Slavonic, Germanic and Greek languages. The development of l>r was natural. The path taken by the word over thousands of years was accompanied by phonetic reactions, the majority of which are already well understood and documented.

The Germanic authors of the word kept a hold of the *armed man* group for a considerable period. Its name gave rise to words that have become the names of kings (**luj**), great reformers (**luter**) and terms with characteristic meanings (**lider**).

However, the importance of this meeting with the Sumerian lulu and lu-ti (lu-tir) also lay in the fact that now we can build a system of identical relations: *doubled = multiplied by an arrow:*

ma-ma = ma-ti, ma-ter
pa-pa = pati, pater

Doubling meant not only an increase, but an elevation as well. Simply a woman or a man, together creating descendants, were named unequivocally, as accepted in modern Chinese: **ma** and **fu**.

And mama and mater, papa and pater are the great Ma and the great Pa. This was achieved through use of the *multiplication (increasing) arrow*, which, in the majority of scriptures of the time was named, it appears, with a Sumerian word and only in a few, with a pre-Sumerian *j.

Compare: ma-ma= maj – *mother* (Portuguese)

papa = paj – *pater, father* (Portuguese)

I would class the plural ending in Slavonic languages – i/j among this number. In a number of Turkic languages this role is fulfilled by the suffix **–ter/tar.**

… Thus, we are considering known hieroglyphs that mean *human* (Sumerian 𐀀 , ancient Chinese ➤ and the previously unknown ⊒). We have seen that the Sumerians obtained the meaning *people* by doubling the sign for *human* (𐀀 𐀀); the pre-Latin people, by adding multiplication lines (⊟). Using this experience as an analogy and allowing for the results of linguistic analysis, success has been achieved in recreating a hypothetical group of signs 𐀀 ↑ (𐀀 |), that replaced the doubling. Chinese script was unable to apply a graphic multiplication factor such as in Indoeuropean languages and the concept of *people* was expressed descriptively as *human-many*.

The Indoeuropeans and the Turkic people used the *multiplicating (increasing) arrow* in their grammar as a formant of the plural.

These examples bear witness to the fact that before the arrival of the ancient Semites in Meopotamia, a multi-ethnic culture resided there, within which there were Indoeuropeans. And Turkic peoples, which I would like to cover in my essay *The Turkic Pyramid.*

THE TURKIC PYRAMID

Over the years of my studies of the Turkisms I have encountered in the vocabularies of living and extinct languages, an image of history has formed in my consciousness, akin to the Greek letter alpha: **A**. The crossing line divides the visible part of the biography of the ethnos from the unseen foundations, which stretch into the darkness of the endless past. And yet it is in the unseen foundations of the pyramid that the most interesting part of Turkic history is found, in which the Turkic people are revealed as one of the most creatively active peoples of early humanity. The words they have left in Sumerian, Ancient Egyptian, in the languages of ancient Europe, ancient India, Iran, China and South America (Maians, Incas, Aztecs) speak of an advanced culture of the Turkic people compared with those ethnoses, in the language (and scripture) of which incredibly indicative traces of influence have remained.

A number of examples bear witness to the contribution of the proto-Turks in the development of ideas of sun worship. Without material from Turkic vocabularies the etymology of the main signs of the Sun and their names, which reached us in the ancient scriptures found by archaeologists, would simply be impossible:

➤ - **ud** – *sun*, ⊕ · **udu** – *god of the sun* (Sumerian); ⊙ - **Ra** – *god of the sun* (Ancient Egypt) ; ⊙ - *sun* (ancient Chinese); ▣ - **kiŋ (king, kin)** – *sun* (Maia); **D** - **jaj** – *sun* (Old Turkic)

In Old Turkic alphabetic script, which reached Mongolia and Altai and which can be detected on stone stelae of the 7th-8th centuries BCE, the first hieroglyphs of the pre-Sumerian style (i.e. without diacritical additions) are still preserved, such as ⩜ **äb'** - *home*, **D jaj** – 1) *sun*; 2) *onion* and others. Used separately, they expressed an entire word; applied together with other signs they designated only a sound: **b', j** – in the presented examples.

The similarity of certain ancient Turkic letters with Sumerian hieroglyphs makes us believe in the incredible longevity of the forms and meanings of the most ancient graphemes and make us use them when analysing the complex hieroglyphs of that era.

The Sumerian hieroglyph ▷ **ud** – sun is afforded a large article in *1001 Words,* where we intend to name and examine words, obtained by authors of new words from the names of signs of the so-called *Sumerian Carousel:* ※.

The name of the sign **ud** when changing its position by 90° and 180° changed accordingly. Both in form and in meaning. Authors of words used this technique in several scriptures of that time. Here we are looking at the etymology of only one, the starting sign of the *carousel* - **ud**. Its archetype, reflected in several *flipped* and *turned* forms, is subjected to analysis.

* ▷ ▷ **ud – sun**

The archetype was a compound sign, comprised of the simple **X** and ▷. The second component appears in Sumerian script as ▷ **u** – *ten, a ten*. The first did not survive until our time: the oblique cross was not mentioned in the limited repertoire of the first hieroglyphs, discovered in a clay tablets, dug from hills near the Arabic settlement of Babil (at one time Babylon). However, knowing the name of the Angle, using algebraic logic, we separate the name of another element from ud: **X -*d.**

What transpires is that the Sumerian author of words applied Rule 2 of the first hieroglyphic grammar (*if you combine signs, combine their names, too*): ▷ **ud.**

However, an important contradiction arises here, which is impossible to avoid: the Sume-rians wrote in a horizontal line, only **from left to right**.[16] And if they (the Sumerians) had creat-ed this combination of simple signs, it would have read as - * **du.**

This sacred sign, so important for the sun worshippers, was created by those who wrote **from right to left.**

---

[16] Čestmír Loukotka *Razvitiye* pis'ma 1950. M. p. 36

... The ancient Turkic peoples in the 8th century CE wrote with a horizontal line from right to left. This is a statement of evident fact. However, when the genuine antiquity of Turkic scripture is finally proven, we will also assert the following: in the 3rd millennium before the Common Era, the Turkic people had preserved the horizontal line and its direction from right to left. And the first fact in the system of proof of this position will be the positioning and the reading of the simple signs in the compound Sumerian **ud** – *sun*. The following elements also survived in the Ancient Turkic alphabet: ➤ **u (o), X – di**. It was these that a priest of a pre-Turkic tribe brought together into the archetype ➤ - *****u-di.**

Then the law of synharmonism intervened in proceedings, controlling (or having always controlled?) the Turkic word. In other words, a progressive assimilation of the quality of sound. More simply, the quality of the starting syllable spread to the subsequent syllables. Simpler still, if the first sound is hard, the subsequent sounds are hardened as well. Both vowels and consonants. Therefore, if the first is **u** (hard), then **di** (soft) unavoidably turns into **d** (hard): * **u – di > ud.**

And it is in this form that the pre-Turkic sign for the sun and its name were adopted by the Sumerians. This points to the particular relationships between these ethnoses at that time: for a people to replace their name for the sacred celestial body with one brought from outside, the newcomers really had to try to do something special.

And what they did was to try to bring the ideology of sun worship to the pagan environment of Mesopotamia, where the main divinity was seen as Venus, the evening star.

The pre-Turkic peoples came to Mesopotamia in two tribes, which explains the two variations of the sign of the Sun, included in the Sumerian script. And used in closely related meanings: ➤ - **ud (ut)** 1) *sun;* 2)* *cow;* 3) * *fire.* ⊕ - **udu (utu)** – 1) *God of the Sun* 2) *ram* (a solar animal, like the Cow, calf or Ox).

The culture of one tribe recognised the sign of the Full Moon and the sign of negation - the Straight Cross (* ✝ - *shiny dot*), while the other culture recognised the Northern Moon and the Oblique Cross (* ✕ - *shiny dot*).

We will speak in more detail about the signs of the Sun ☉ - ⊕ - ⊕ and ⊕ ⊕ ▷ in *1001 Words*, particularly about the birth of the Holy Cross and future Christianity. And about the symbol for Islam – the Star in the Crescent Moon.

And about the names of the gods of the Indoeuropean ethnoses, brought from Ancient Western Asia.

... The ancestors of the Latin people read the combination ▷ from left to right: *di-u. The Indoeuropeans, in an attempt to understand the genesis of the Latin **deūs** – *god*, first separated the root **deu** (**-us** is an indicator of the masculine gender, although the name of a single god could not have gender endings; this was only possible in the pagan polytheism). The archetype - *di-u. This is nearer to the Luwian **Tivas** – *sun god* (Asia Minor, 2nd millennium BCE) and the following form in neighbouring Hittite: **Šivas** – *god*. Old Indian **dev** – *god*, without the gender ending. However, the Supreme God **Diavus-pitar** – *God the Father* (*Dev-us-piter) still retains the Latin masculine ending, which we spoke of earlier. This is in the same way as the Romans during Christianity retained the version of the name without a gender ending in their folklore - Ju-piter. Where j-u = di-u – *god of the sun* (j=di).

This is covered in more detail in *1001 Words*.

In an expanded study of the *Turkic Pyramid*, complete chapters should appear: *Turkic people in Sumeria, Turkic people in Ancient Egypt, Turkic people in Etruria, Turkic people in Ancient India, Turkic people in Ancient China,* which reinforce the foundations of the pyramid with specific material.

Using this same system one could construct a pyramid of history for every ethnos, once great and now of lesser importance. The peaks of some are sharp-pointed, like the Egyptian pyramids, while others are flat-topped, like the stepped pyramids of Mesopotamia. In many the peaks did not reach the line that separated the visible part of history from the unexplored; in some it barely protrudes and in others still the outline of history is similar to an upturned pyramid, or the mushroom cloud of a nuclear explosion.

If we adhere to alphabetical order, the Dictionary should open with etymologies of words that begin with *a*. However, such a principle is not suitable for *1001 Words*. We will begin with words derived from the first names for Bull – Moon **müŋ** (M-Dialect) and **bůŋ** (B-Dialect).

Under any a we encounter b and m. I would help in the creation of the *Avar Pyramid*, in memory of my friends, Rasul Gamzatov and Magomet Aliyev. The Avar vocabulary contains words of incredible antiquity, which retain a description of the sign in their semantics. For example, ber – 1) *eye*; 2) *wheel*.[17] In essence, these two words are homonyms, the former names of the first hieroglyphs, which differed from one another only in the form of one element, which can be recovered:

⊙ **ber** - *eye*
◉ **ber** - *wheel*

The first meanings were linked with the image of the sun.

The Turkic people saw the sign of the eye and transposed the common name to the element, the Point. This is probably how the first unit in Turkic script came to appear. [Cp.] **ber** – *one* (Tat., Bash.), **per** (Chuv.), **bir** (Turkish, Az., Kaz., Uz., Kirg., Kum., Turkm., Gag., Kara-kalpak), **pir** (Khak., Alt., Tuv.)

The *mountain* and *forest* languages, just like the permafrost, preserve the dinosaurs and mammoths of vocabulary that have long since died out in other, too sociable dialects. The etymologist would do well to take this feature of the geography of language into account.

THE CODE OF THE WORD
(a brief course)

So let's clarify the meaning of the term the *code of the word:* it is a collection of key rules, according to which the first words were created and these words became entrenched with the subsequent practice as the languages developed. The rules of word creation were effective and were actively used until while the priests interpreted the sacred symbols of their communi-ties. These symbols served as phylactery-type crests, upon which the fate of a tribe or clan was dependent and they were preserved for a considerable time. Their contents were interpreted if the first values had been lost.

ONOMATOPAEIA
(The simple symbols of moon worship)

The first words used by homo sapiens were most likely of onomatopoeic origin.

Man made the second step toward language, schematically depicting a *talking* animal. His congeners, seeing a drawn wavy line, understood that the subject related to a snake and they named the drawing to correspond with the name it gave itself: ∾∾∾ – š-š (s-s) – *snake*. And if they saw – ⌣ mů-ů-ůŋ (bů-ů-ůŋ) – *bull*.

Of the unvoiced items a projectile weapon was named onomatopoeically – *ha! – the sharp sound made by a spear or a stone as it flies through the air. And the symbol was depicted: **|** (•) – ha! – *spear (stone)*.

SIGN SYMBOLISM
(From simple signs to compound signs)

The first religion, moon worship, was born in Africa in the equatorial zone, where the young moon appears like a small boat or cup. However, primitive man (the priest) first saw the Golden Horns of the black sacred bull. Therefore hehave the Moon the same name under which he earlier knew this large beast.

Rule 1 **(R-1):**

> **Transfer the name of a symbol to an object that is similar to a graphic or natural symbol.**

∪ mů-ů-ůŋ (bů-ů-ůŋ) – 1) Bull, 2) Moon, month.

This experience is also applied to other symbols which, over time, were to acquire a poly-sematic nature (multiple meanings):

∾∾∾ – š-š (s-s) – 1) Snake; 2) river, stream; 3) water; 4) hills; 5) land and so on.

The age had arrived of words with an artificial origin, meaning manmade, **onomatopoeic** words.

This age has continued until the present day. Thanks to R-1, all items and phenomena from the world around us and from the abstract will be given names.

The most intensive process of onomatopoeic word creation took place in the period of the functioning of the figurative script (the proto-heiroglyph). The multiple meaning of the diagrammatic, figurative symbols enabled priests over the tens of thousands of years of development of Homo Sapiens, to give rise to millions of words from the names of a few simple and two-syllable signs.

CHANGE IN FAITH.
THE BIRTH OF THE COMPOUND SYMBOL

Man crosses the waters that separate Africa from Europe. This is today's northern coast of the Mediterranean Sea, where sun worship was to be born. For the first sun worshippers the previous deity (the Moon) was now an unhallowed, rejected celestial body. When forming the sign for the new deity, the priest ascribed significance to a long observed phenomenon: the Sun appears after the Moon has gone out (died). And so the priest formed the first compound sign for the new god:

♀ – *slain Moon - Sun*

The priests of the clans would diversify variations of the sacred sign in the generations that followed:

♀ ♀ ⊖

However, in one tribe, the sun with a tail was replaced with a symbol that is closer to the natural form , where, in place of a spear there is a wound, a hole in the Moon. The meaning is the same – *slain Moon, non-Moon*.

In the coloured version, a red dot is used in place of a hole:

☉ – *bloody wound of the Moon > slain Moon*.

This colour of the wound was not preserved in all tribes; the spot became black in many.

The meaning of the spot changes (*wound, stone* and others), but the name was to be preserved the same for a considerable time: ***ha!** – 1) spear; 2) wound; 3) stone, as the common meaning of this symbol is that of *death*.

When the bow was invented in one of the tribes (and this occurred during the time of sun worship, when different clans adopted the emblems Ψ, contamination of which eventually led to the invention of the bow and arrow) the *arrow*-**j*, in the scripture of this tribe came to replace the traditional spear -**ha*. The symbol remains the same, with a line (horizontal or vertical). The name of the arrow switched to the sign of the *stone (point)* and *wound (circle)*, with the same weapon, *death, no* and *diminution* preserved in the new name. With time the merging of tribes would lead to a combining of writing traditions. The common grammar found a place for both *ha and *j in close or even opposite functions.

***Rule 2* (R-2)** – this is a continuation of the previous rule:

> **The name of a sign is transferred to an item or phenomenon that is similar to it, only in diminutive form.**

This clarification came considerably later, when the formants were deprived of their previously categorical nature and referred in diminutive form, rather than fully negating.

***Rule 3* (R-3):**

> **If you combine signs, combine their names, too.**

♀ ♀ ⊙ ⊙ ⊙ – 1) můŋ -ha (bůŋ-ha); 2) ha-můŋ, (ha-bůŋ). This is an external inflex-ional combination.

However, there was also an internal inflexional combination: 3) můhaŋ (bůhaŋ) = mhaůŋ (bhaůŋ) = mhaŋ (bhaŋ).[18]

---

[18] Internal flexion – an ingenious invention by the priest, hinted at by the placing of the subordinate symbol inside the primary symbol. *And the name of the subordinate symbol shall be inside the name of the primary symbol.*

Later, when the spear (ha) was understood in other tribes as an arrow (j) and, accordingly, the flexion (the name of the official symbol) changed: 1) můŋ -j (bůŋ-j); 2) j- můŋ (j- bůŋ); 3) men (beŋ)=miŋ (biŋ).

As the first compound signs consisted of two elements, one of which stood for death (negation), this official sign *ha (*j) would later be used for all other functions. This how the grammar of negation was formed.

As the tribes increased in number so did the variations of the sacred sign of the Sun, where anti-variations of the sign of the Moon were used:

O ∪ V

The future table of signs for the Sun would include derivatives of these three main signs for the Moon:

I. ♀ ♀ ♀ ⊖ ⊙ ⊙ ⊙
II. Ψ Ψ Ψ ⊕ ⌣ ⋃ ⋃ Ɗ Ǝ Ɔ etc.
III. Y Ψ ∀ ⍌ V V ▷ ⋧ ⋗ ⋗

The sacred signs for the Sun and the *animals of the Sun* (the non-Bulls – Cow, Ram, Calf, Ox and others) became the emblems of the tribes of an ever-multiplying humankind. They were passed from generation to generation and the priests, the keepers of the Sign, adopted the emblem in objects, ornaments, pennants and so on, and using them in myths and legends. Attempts made to diversify the mythology surrounding the sacred symbols in all their finer detail that were handed down through the generations forced the priests to elaborate Rule 4 (R-4), using this same grammar of negation.

For example, the Slavs who had lived in the Mediterranean area borrowed the main hieroglyph of Ancient Egypt **Ra** – *God of the Sun.* Judging by the words obtained from this name, the Slav tribes saw two or three variations of this sign – with a red spot (wound) and with a hole. However at that time they did not encounter the hieroglyph with a black spot (in the second or first millennium BCE).

Let us look more closely at ⊙ **Ra.**

Rule 4 (**R-4**):

> **To give an item of a compound sign a name, negate its overall name.**

At that time the Slavs already used the negative **ni** and **no**. This was how the name of the red spot was obtained, understood at that time as a *little sun* – * Ra-no > **rano** – *morning* (Czech), **ранок** [ranok] – *morning* (Ukrainian). In the Russian, three words became established from three dialects: **рано** [rano – *early*], **рань** [ran' – *early-morning hour*] and **рана** [rana – *wound*]. And there was a fourth, where the distinguishing formant was used prepositionally: **нора** [nora – *burrow*].

Thus:

☉ - 1) Ra-no; 2) Ra-na; 3) Ra-ni
◉ - 1) no- Ra

The Germanic languages also used the negation: *'j > *dži > **di**. Given the meaning of the words, derived from the name of the spot *Ra-di > ... all words with the meaning red in the Germanic languages originate from this archetype: Rot (German), red (English). Откуда the Romantic languages have rosso (Italian), moude (French). In Latin and in certain Romantic languages, the meanings of words that stem from *Ra-'j > Ra-di characteristically change and point to a different structure of the sign.

In Spanish **rayo** – *ray* is the form that precedes the Latin ***radi** – *ray*. With a different generic ending, the Spanish word even more accurately describes the sign of negation: **ra ya** – 1) *dash, line*; 2) *strip* (in a field); 3) *parting* (in the hair); 4) *border, boundary* etc. It is from here that we get **radius** – *a straight line, running from the centre of a circle* (Latin).

A variation of sign is recovered: ♀ **ra**, from which we obtain the name of the negation dash, understood as a ray and a radius: ♀ *-ra-di *a straight line, running from the centre of a circle*)

***Rule 5* (R-5):**

> **To name the other part of a two-part sign, negate the name of the previous part.**

This technique came to be used rather late, when the sign of the Sun had acquired abstract meanings, such as country and nation. For example:

⊙ Ra – *country, nation*. In the centre – the Sovereign. ⊙ 1) **re** – *king* (Italian), **rex** (Latin) (The spot was most likely still red). The external inflexional formation *Ra-j' found its place in Ancient Indian **raja**, meaning *king* (**-a** – masculine ending) and in Semitic **rais** – *head* (Arabic), reš – head (Phoenician) For now R-4 applies.

Finally, R-5: ⊙ – **re-j – *kingdom* (preserved in the German **Reih**). The external inflexional **rajo** – *king* (**-o** – masculine, in the Romantic languages), **rajo-n** – *kingdom* (in the Germanic there is a regressive assimilation of quality: **rejon > rehjon** – *region*).

I have verified all Five Rules of the grammar of negation in etymological practice, the results of which will be included in the Universal Etymological Dictionary *1001 Words*.

From the time I worked on *AZ-i-IA* (1975) I know well the reaction of scholarly readers to my exercises in etymology. Those who earn a living teaching the postulates of linguistics flick through the brochure to convince themselves yet again that I am dabbling in matters that are not my own. A few of them who care to take a closer, less hasty look at the lesson, who read it and dwell on it, will be able to understand.

The tree of linguistics is not a tree at all, but a wizened stump without roots. One can hang all manner of loudspeakers and bright lights on it, but they will never replace living fruit. Restore the root system of language and the dried plant will come back to life – the plant that, in its essence, is the tree of life of the tribe known as Homo Sapiens.

And *1001 Words* will help this process on its way.

Any reader, even of just this concluding chapter of the introduction, can test this collection of rules (or some of them) to reveal the genesis of words from their own native language. If such tests are indeed performed, I would be delighted to learn of them and agree with or contest the obtained results. I have set up a special e-mail address for this purpose, suleimenov.1001@gmail.com, and the best of them will be included in the *1001 Words*.

It's motto shall be the Italian proverb *Tutto il mondo e'paesa!* meaning *All the World is one big village*. The word *paesa* is also translated as country. Perhaps the poetry of science could one day unite the world of the Homo Sapiens.

www.ingramcontent.com/pod-product-compliance
Lightning Source LLC
Chambersburg PA
CBHW020659300426
44112CB00007B/456